Take Time

A Book of Meditations

By Rev. Raymond Harms

Concordia Publishing House

First Printing April 2011

Concordia Publishing House. All rights reserved. No part of this book may be reserved or reproduced in any manner whatsoever without written permission of the publisher, except in the case of brief quotations in articles and reviews.

Printed in the United States of America

For information on the content of this book, please write:

    Rev. Raymond Harms
    239 Logelin Drive
    Reedsburg, Wisconsin 53959.

Dedication

This book is dedicated to my friend, Vern Austin, who saved my life while fishing.

Acknowledgements

I am truly appreciative of all the time and energy that Barb Teig has given to the proofreading of these articles. Barb had her hands full working with what I have written and her advice is truly appreciated. I also thank my wife Ione who has done much typing to help put these articles before you. Along with Barb and Ione, I acknowledge my son-in-law John Suguitan for his assistance with the page layout and publishing of this book.

Foreword

For the past 18 years I have been writing articles for various newspapers under the title Take Time. Here are some 170 articles chosen for you to Take Time and spend some quality time in rest and meditation. My friend Vern Austin spent some quality time with me while fishing, after he had pulled me back into the boat. I had passed out from exhaustion, working too hard doing the work of the Call that God had given me. My priority was work and I was not getting enough rest or time with my family. A reader out in Maine, after reading these articles, wrote a letter suggesting I assemble these articles for rest and relaxation and some quality time with God. Though there are a large number not included in this book, the devotions I've selected are just the beginning.

These articles are not meant for a theological definition on any subject, but only for some guidance in thinking through a difficult situation. These articles were born out of not only my need, but also the needs of the many people with whom I served.

Sit back, relax in some quiet place with God, your Bible and a word from Take Time. This is well worth the health of your body, mind and soul.

Lent
When AFRAID

In most lives there is a time when we become "afraid." For example, some experience fear when taking a new job, moving to a new neighborhood, going to a new school, entering marriage, upon hearing of a terminal disease, when faced with death itself, when things go wrong in our lives, and so the list could go on. If we have no one to whom we can turn, if we have no place to go, if we have nothing in which we find solace, our fear can be most terrifying. We offer the following from Holy Scripture to which you can turn when you experience something new or different or numbing in your life.

When afraid, turn to the Holy Scripture and read the following: Psalm 23; Psalm 27; Psalm 34:4; Matthew 10:28; Matthew 20:28; Philippians 4:13; Hebrews 13:5-6. These passages are but a few from the Holy Bible that can offer you strength and peace when afraid.

One that is a particular favorite of mine is Philippians 4:13: "I can do all things through Christ Who strengthens me." No matter if it is a matter of health, a new location and people among whom we live, the announcement by the doctor of a serious or terminal illness, new work, or whatever it may be in your life, Christ is there to give the necessary strength to do what must be done. Along with this is Matthew 28:20: "...And surely, I am with you always, to the very end of the age." The Psalmist said, "The Lord is my light and my salvation, whom shall I fear?" (Psalm 27:1). The most beloved Psalm of all is Psalm 23:1,4: "The Lord is my Shepherd,

I shall not want...yes, even though I walk through the valley of the shadow of death, I will fear no evil, for You are with me. Your rod and your staff, they comfort me." Hebrew 13:6 says: "So we say with confidence, 'The Lord is my helper; I will not be afraid. What can man do to me?" How beautiful God's own Word is for us when we are afraid!

Turn to the Lord often, especially when you are afraid, and let Him comfort you. There is nothing in life that can take God's own peace away from us. May God give you strength and calmness of heart to live each day in the Lord without fear. During this Holy week Take Time to follow the way of the cross and learn of Jesus the Way, the Truth, and the Life. Herein lies the secret to conquering all fears in life!

ANXIOUS

In our hurried lives of the "modern" age, we are pressured about many things. Our lives are troubled by money, jobs, friends, and worry about what people think and we lose sleep, have ulcers, and become miserable to be around. The question before us is "How can we find peace?" This is the time to turn to God's Word and listen to God speak with us about His way for peace and happiness.

The following are a few of the many passages from God's Word which will help us: Psalm 46; 107; 121; 139; Matthew 6:19-34; Luke 17; Philippians 4:6; 1 Peter 5:6-7. Read these references and then concentrate on Philippians 4:6, which says: "Do not be anxious about anything, but in everything, by prayer and petition, with thanksgiving, present your requests to God." The Lord presents a simple solution to a serious problem, namely, take it to Him in prayer. You are invited to spell out your anxious feeling in detail and request of God His aid and counsel. Jesus said, "Whatsoever you ask the Father in my name, He will give it to you." John 16:23. We are to place no conditions on the requests we bring to God. We are simply to name them and ask God to resolve them. Jesus says He shall do that, but, in His time and manner.

In fulfillment of our commitment to God we can always turn to a good Friend. We sing

"What a Friend we have in Jesus,
All our sins and griefs to bear,
What a privilege to carry
Everything to God in prayer.

Oh what peace we often forfeit,
Oh what needless pain we bear,
All because we do not carry
Everything to God in prayer.

God means every Word He has spoken, and He cares very much for you. If you find this hard to believe read Psalm 139 and find out how much you mean to God. He knows all about you. You need only confide in Him, and He will take care of those anxious thoughts and concerns of your life. You do matter to the Lord Jesus. We need but only turn to Him, trust Him and find our rest.

Lent

Good

Today we are hearing more and more people experience life by being bitter and critical. How unhappy they must be! Our Lord speaks to this in His holy Word. Read the following: Luke 6:27-49; 1 Corinthians 13; 2 Corinthians 4; Ephesians 4. Again, these are but a few of God's many words to help us find true happiness. The opposite of being bitter and critical is to love. The Lord said for us to love even our enemies when He said: "You shall love your neighbor as yourself." Maybe this is the problem for someone who is bitter and critical: they don't love themselves.

1 Corinthians 13 is God's definition of love. When all can live together in this manner, we will see the good in everyone. The story is told of a religious group that had the custom at the burial of a family member or acquaintance to say something good before leaving the grave and burial. The person who had died had been a scoundrel, to say the least. In the cold winds of the prairie winter all waited for someone to say something good, but no one could think of anything to say. Finally in the sub-zero weather, standing on the wind side of the group, an elderly woman said, "He had a mother." The clergy said "Amen" and they left for the warmth of their cars and home. It may not sound like much, but that was something good.

No doubt we all know of someone so angry that they can't find something good to say. God says, "love is patient, love is kind, it remembers no wrong, it forgives." Jesus, on the cross, said of those who crucified and reviled Him, "Father, forgive them, for they know not what they do." Should anything less be said by us of those around us if forgiveness is warranted for a wrong? Reading 1 Corinthians 13 and Psalm 139 can help all to feel better about one's self and those around us. Looking at the cross as we begin Lent, should we not say, "How has He loved us?" Also, it is written, "Greater love has no one than this, that one lay down his life for a friend (and enemy)."

May those who are bitter and critical and may all who are not critical and bitter find the love of God to be the source of strength and true happiness in Christ Jesus, our Lord and Savior. Take Time to enjoy life by finding the good, it's there.

Post Easter
Bored

Perhaps we have not taken a good look at a real Christian for a long time because life has become so routine and habitual, thus, boring. A.W. Toner once wrote: "A real Christian is an odd number, anyway. He feels supreme love for One Whom he has never seen; talks familiarly every day to Someone he cannot see; expects to go to heaven on the virtue of Another; empties himself in order to be full; admits he is wrong so he can be declared right; goes down in order to get up; is strongest when he is weakest; richest when he is poorest and happiest when he feels the worst. He dies so he can live; forsakes in order to have; gives away so he can keep; sees the invisible; hears the inaudible; and knows that which passeth knowledge." Now, how can one be bored with this king of life?

You are invited to open your Bible and read the following passages concerning boredom: 2 Kings 5; Job 38; Psalm 103 and 104; and Ephesians 3. These are just a few words from God to help you through the experience of being bored. Take Time to examine yourself and see if what God says and Toner illustrates might be a solution for you. The disciples never found life boring being around Jesus, and neither will you. Your age doesn't make a difference when you sit at the feet of Jesus.

During this post-Easter season Take Time on Sunday and worship by walking with Jesus. You are guaranteed life will never be boring because He will always have something to do for you in your family, in your neighborhood, in your community, in ways of helping others through service, in school, in your church, and so the list goes on. Read 1 Corinthians 13, the love chapter. God's definition of the real meaning of love and life will open like a beautiful flower around you and you will never be bored.

Caring

How much do you care about the people around you? How much do you care about those who are sick, lonely, alone, the "outcast," the homeless, the separated? The list goes on and on. Caring is important to all of us. Besides Christian congregations, there are help groups which are very important because of what they provide to help those facing a very difficult time or are nearing the end of their life. And, yet, there are many who don't know about the caring and the help available for them. We have opportunity to reach out to take their hand and walk with them. The big problem is that many don't know of the care, the help, and the love that waits for them as they walk through this time of life with great difficulty.

Home health and Hospice groups, to designate in general just a couple of agencies, work with the personal doctor(s), nurse(s), and clergy as support and help in the home and in a few nursing homes along with other support groups. This is to strengthen the quality of life for each individual in difficult and some terminal conditions. In addition nursing services are there to help all who have everyday health conditions that need special attention and care. Other help agencies are present to help people of all ages and color in their need. We think of the Lord's words in Matthew referring to people's needs: "I was sick and you visited me; hungry and you fed me; naked and you clothed me; in prison and you visited me; homeless and you took me in." We all are called upon to love those in need and these are a few ways to demonstrate care, concern, and love for those in need. Our example is Jesus, who was always there to help.

A real problem for many is that they are not aware of the help that is waiting for them. Your doctor or your clergy know, call them. Here is a demonstration of the love of Jesus and those who follow Him for whomever would have such need. It is in keeping with the Holy Bible's words "to love your neighbor." Take Time to love and be loved; Take Time to care; Take Time to be cared for; and Take Time to love one another. The rewards are incredible, God-pleasing and rewarding and very fulfilling.

Deliverer

Take time for Jesus, your DELIVERER. So often we hear it said, "I just don't have time for _____." We are so busy in this life that we don't take time for our spouse, our children, our brothers and sisters, our friends, and most important of all, our Lord and Savior, Jesus Christ. In America, we have been so blest by God with abundance in everything and with everything. The other day I saw some college students from Russia walking through one of our major store chains. They were stopping and looking at different items and pointing at the prices talking excitedly. My thought was "Are we taking all things for granted here in America?" Perhaps we are so used to having all this abundance of things around us. Even Americans at the poverty level have more money than citizens in third-world countries.

This is a good time for our inventory of life. While we live with abundance all around us, let us "Take Time to smell the roses," and truly enjoy living. We can begin at the feet of Jesus as did Mary, who along with her brother Lazarus and sister Martha, loved Him dearly as a friend. Not long after the encounter of Jesus with Mary and Martha, Jesus was told that His friend Lazarus was sick unto death. The Bible says "Jesus wept" at what He observed around Him. He delivered Mary and Martha from the loss of their brother by raising him from the dead.

There are many other examples of the love of Jesus: The Lepers, the man crippled from birth, the tax collector, Peter's mother-in-law and her poor health condition, the woman taken in adultery, the people of Jerusalem, the little children, the woman who had an ailment that could not be healed by human hands, and so the list could go on and on. All show us a great and deep love by Jesus for people. We fit right in with all of our pain and suffering and tears and concerns and hopes and dreams.

Let us commit ourselves together with our loved ones to the Lord in continuous prayer. Let us Take Time to know who our loved ones truly are in their uniqueness as individuals. If you have a burden known to all or known only by yourself, take it to the Lord in prayer and He shall answer you as He promised with a resounding "Yes," "No," or "Not Yet." Leave which answer it will be up to Him and accept His decision that will lead you yet to the next step of life. St. Paul said: "All things work together for the good of them that love God." (Romans 8:28). We may not always understand, but let us trust Him and we shall be "delivered."

Discouraged

Take Time when you are DISCOURAGED to find some peace of mind and heart and being. Discouragement comes into every person's life whether young or old, rich or poor. It can drain you of every ounce of energy that one may have throughout life if left unchecked. It affects everyone around you. Those around you can detect discouragement in your voice, your face, your posture, and your words.

Discouragement can be discerned at every age. Little children may start with their thumbs in their mouth, or, their going off to a place of safety for them, or they become either very quiet or very loud or very angry, or they cling to their parent's leg and so on. The behavior of children in relation to discouragement is not much different than that of an adult. Adults may not suck their thumb or cling to someone's leg, but they do have some "escape hatch" to a problem they have. So, what can you do?

One experiencing discouragement can become involved in some activity: someone to speak with, read a book, work in the garden, play a game of golf (or go to a driving range and hit a couple of buckets of balls thinking of what has discouraged them), go for a long and healthy walk. Jesus, when He was faced with a similar challenge, would go to a quiet place and pray; He would spend time with His disciples, speak with children, find the "rejected" of society and share with them His attention and love, or go to the house of God to worship Him and commune with Him.

How we can successfully handle matters that discourage us today hasn't changed much. Let me offer some suggestions for reading God's Holy Word, the Holy Bible,. Read any one or all of the following references: Psalms 23, 42, 43, 55:22; or Isaiah 40; or Matthew 5:11-12; or 2 Corinthians 4:8-18; or Philippians 4:4-7. You can find a quiet place and meditate and pray. Or change your outlook like a young boy who had just started baseball. He couldn't hit the ball. One day his mother overheard and then watched her son. The boy would throw the ball in the air and then swing and miss. This was repeated three times equaling three outs as in a real ball game. The mother then heard her little boy say: "See, I told you that I was a good pitcher, I struck out three batters with just nine pitches." This little boy wouldn't take "no" for an answer and neither should we.

Let this suggestion be for you. Find somewhere to be alone. Then, take your Bible and read one or all of the before afore mentioned Bible readings and meditate on them, sayings to yourself "Now, what is in this reading that is meant for me?" Next, pray if you can. Then find some good listener and speak with them, perhaps going on a long walk together. Remember, you "can do all things through Christ (Jesus) Who strengthens you (me)."

DISSATISFIED

A story is told of Jesus and His disciples walking one day along a stony road. Jesus asked each of them to choose a stone to carry for Him. John chose a large one while Peter chose the smallest. Jesus then led them then to the top of a mountain and commanded that the stones be made into bread. Each disciple, by this time tired and hungry, was allowed to eat the bread which he held in his hand, but of course Peter's was not sufficient to satisfy his hunger. John gave him some of his.

Some time later Jesus again asked the disciples to pick up a stone to carry. This time Peter chose the largest of all. Taking them to a river, Jesus told them to cast the stones into the water. They did so, but looked at one another in bewilderment. "For whom," asked Jesus, "did you carry the stone?"

Do we get the message? Why do we do things in our lives? Is it for self-gratification, for praise, for honor, for glory, for bigger, or better than the "Jones"? If we act out of using the talents and gifts God gave us, we will find contentment, even if it is not the wealth and happiness others seemingly have. For some divine light on this matter, let us turn to God's Word and listen to His counsel. St. Paul spoke at God's direction: "I know how to live when I am poor, and I know how to live when I have plenty. I have learned the secret of being happy at any time in everything that happens, when I have enough to eat and when I go hungry, when I have more than I need and when I do not have enough. I can do all things through Christ, because He gives me strength." (Philippians 4:12-13). St. Matthew said, "Those who want to do right more than anything else are happy, because God will fully satisfy them." (Matthew 5:6). Here are some further readings from the Holy Bible for you to TAKE TIME and find satisfaction: Jeremiah 31:14; Joel 2:26; Psalm 63:1-5; Psalm 103:1-5; 2 Corinthians 9:8. How good God is to us! TAKE TIME to count your blessings as God sees them, not as "man" sees them.

The hymn writer wrote:

O Lord, my God, when I in awesome wonder;

Consider all the works Thy hand hath made,

I see the stars, I hear the mighty thunder,

Thy pow'r throughout the universe displayed;

Then sings my soul, my Savior, God, to Thee.

How great Thou art!....

Forgiveness

Forgiveness is perhaps the most difficult experience a person has in life. Sins against us vary in "degree" as we perceive them, though not in God's experience. To God, sin is sin and there are no degrees. The Bible tells us that Christ came into this world to die for sin and that matters not which commandment was broken and so act accordingly in a way that does not please the Lord God of heaven and earth.

Joseph, of the Old Testament of the Bible, was a young boy sold by his envious and jealous brothers into slavery where he suffered great agony and pain. Later in life Joseph, who had been elevated to the position of great power in Egypt, had the occasion to "pay back" for the wrongs done to him. Instead, he chose to forgive them.

Corrie ten Boom tells of a time in her life when she was face to face with one of her former prison guards from the concentration camps of World War II. The man, after hearing her message but not recognizing her, came to her and expressed the peace he felt in his heart upon hearing of God's great forgiving love for all people. He wanted personal assurance from Corrie that this forgiveness was his. She thought quietly to herself that in no way could she nor would she forgive this man. But, when she wanted to leave, she felt a certain presence flow through her to this man as she expressed God's and her forgiveness to him. The man left in peace never knowing with whom he had spoken. Corrie, too, felt a great peace that she hadn't felt since before WWII.

Has someone wronged you, and you feel great pain? Remember the words of St. Paul to the Christians of Colossae. He said: "Get along with each other, and forgive each other. If someone does wrong to you, forgive that person because the Lord forgave you." (Colossians 3:13). Isaiah said: "The Lord says, 'Forget what happened before, and do not think about the past. I am the one who forgives all your sins, forgive for my sake; I will not remember your sins.'" (Isaiah 43:18,25). Does not swallowing our pride and our hurt make sense? St. Paul said it best to the Romans: "Do not let evil defeat you, but defeat evil by doing good." (Romans 12:21). We can begin the act of forgiveness in prayer to Almighty God for His strength and peace and love. Again, St. Paul: "I can do all things through Him Who gives me strength." (Philippians 4:13).

Let us all so live in peace and love! Herein lies true happiness.

Guilty

We do not like to admit that our sinfulness and rebellion are at the heart of problems of society. We are more comfortable discussing imperfections, weaknesses, mistakes, and errors in judgement. These terms are socially acceptable, and almost everyone identifies with them. But an outright acknowledgment of guilt before a holy God, a 100 percent acceptance of responsibility for wrong doing, runs against our grain. Yet this kind of honesty is the first step to the freedom from sin and guilt that God longs to give us and has provided for us in the death of His Son, Jesus.

The story is told that one day Frederick the Great, King of Prussia, visited a prison and talked with each of the inmates. There were endless tales of innocence, of misunderstood motives, and of exploitation. Finally the king stopped at the cell of a convict who remained silent. "Well," remarked Frederick, "I suppose you are an innocent victim too?" "No, sir, I'm not," replied the man. "I'm guilty and deserve my punishment." Turning to the warden, the king said, "Here, release this rascal before he corrupts all these fine innocent people in here!"

When feeling guilty, confess your guilt to the Lord with sincere acknowledgment of your wrong and He will pardon you. Be honest with yourself and God. St. John said, "But if we confess our sins, He will forgive our sins, because we can trust God to do what is right. He will cleanse us from all the wrongs we have done." (1 John 1:9) The Psalmist said, "Happy is the person whose sins are forgiven, whose wrongs are pardoned." (Psalm 32:1) St. John said of Jesus, "Jesus raised up again and asked her, 'Woman, where are they? Has no one judged you guilty?' She answered. 'No one, sir.' Then Jesus said, 'I also do not judge you guilty. You may go now, but do not sin anymore.'" (John 8:10-11). Read Hebrews 10:22 and live in freedom and know that you are at peace with God. There is a freedom and life waiting for all who would find it with the Lord Jesus Christ. Just TAKE TIME with the Lord and you shall live free in forgiveness. Experience the joy of your risen Lord and Savior, Jesus Christ, who has won the complete victory for you. Be set free to live with Him in peace and no guilt.

Integrity

Integrity appears to be a commodity in short supply today. There are those who live with a double standard. For example, how often have parents said to their children, "You can't watch that movie" and then after the children are in bed, the parents sit down and watch the forbidden movie? Children are told they cannot say certain vulgar words, and then the parents proceed to use them. Children are told they cannot drink alcohol and destroy their health. Parents take their children to Sunday School and leave them, and the parents go their way demonstrating the study of God's Word isn't for them. Then parents wonder where children learn bad living habits and get into trouble.

We look at the morals of our country today. The lessons of the commandments have been taken from the school and instead we teach them the philosophy of the New Age Movement by not giving them a standard to live by, but what they develop from life by their own experience when they have no foundation to build a life of integrity. Marriage has been thrown out by many in preference to living together outside of marriage. More and more children are being raised without God fearing examples. Sad to say, many "Christian churches" today say that this is acceptable and even contributes to this by saying that the sacred Scriptures permit it, or, that the Bible was meant for another age.

It is time for us to all listen to the invitation of Jesus to "Follow Me" as He Himself said. This means to live in love for the Lord, to follow His sacred Word. (IT IS STILL THE ONLY TRUTH!) It means to love your neighbor as yourself. Shakespeare said, "To thine own self be true" and how true this is still today. The Holy Bible says, "Let us draw near with a true heart in full assurance of faith, with our hearts sprinkled clean from an evil conscience and our bodies all our daily lives will surely bring some decency and INTEGRITY back to our everyday lives and restore a morality of love and respect for all. INTEGRITY is the greatest value of all for living.

Work

As one drives or walks down the street, or picks up a newspaper and reads the want ads, we see sign and advertisements seeking workers for their established or beginning business. When one studies the statistics, we find that unemployment is at its lowest for many years. And yet, there are some who are the prime examples of "couch potatoes" saying that the wage offered is too little. A father once told his young son that "if a farmer needs someone to clean his barn, go and do it. It is better to work than to expect a hand out." The lesson to be learned is this from God's holy word: "If any would not work, neither he eat." (2 Thessalonians 3:10). Work provides dignity and self-worth to a person's own image and that of those around them. This may sound harsh in terms of present-day thoughts, but it still is very true.

In almost every instance, one who has found success in the humblest of definitions is one who has started at the bottom and worked his way up to where he is seen as successful. This can mean someone who daily goes to work, brings home a check, provides for family needs, put something away for the future and feels comfortable enough to sleep the whole night through and has peace. The problem for many is that they have to have the biggest and the best and "keep up with the 'Joneses!'" Success is not dollars or things or the people you know. Success is the mark of those who are willing to pay the price of work and achievement in a God-pleasing way. Jesus had no home, no stocks and bonds, etc, nor a savings account in the "money market" (not that these are wrong in and of themselves), but He lived with the right priorities in his life, namely, fulfilling His Father's purpose for Him while here on this earth.

Some of the most successful people (as we define success in our human terminology) are those who live modestly in the humblest of circumstances fulfilling the purpose that God has for them.

Don't you think that we might find something we can learn here from the Master Himself? The way to success is to work hard in life using the gifts God has given us. We each have at least one gift. Until it was time to fulfill His Messianic role in the way of the cross, He worked and lived as a carpenter. What a "role model," don't you think? Remember, the price of success is to Take Time to WORK. It is the Lord's formula for you.

Respect

In working with people of all ages over the years, we have found that a real problem in living is the lack of respect people encounter. When we forget whose we are and who we are, we are confronted with all kinds of problems. For example, when we lose the ability to say who we are, we have no direction in our lives. When we lose respect for ourselves, we look to other sources of encouragement. For example, some turn to overeating, others to alcohol, others to improper relations with regard to the use of their own bodies. When we lose respect for ourselves we no longer set goals and dream dreams positively, and we drift away from other people and lead lonely lives.

We also see what the lack of respect does to the rise of abuse in the home: spousal and/or child. We look at the rise of verbal expressions of the four letter variety and see a good number of insecure people who lack self respect and falsely believe that they have greater stature thereby. Just the opposite is true. We hear more and more of "road rage" and shake our heads in disbelief. What has happened?

There is an answer to the lack of respect if we but turn to the Lord and His Holy Word. One of the greatest Psalms is 139. We have referred to this Psalm often, but feel that the importance of this Psalm needs to be recalled again at this time. Fifty-one times the writer of this chapter uses the personal pronouns I, me, and my in his relationship with God and God with him. This should tell us something special and beautiful, namely, we are important and we do matter to Someone Whose name is God, the great I AM of

Moses' encounter with God at the burning bush on Mt. Sinai. He knows our needs, our hurts, our loneliness, our pain, our suffering, and all our other needs. The writer of the book of Hebrews says we have One "Who is tested in every way as we," (Hebrews 4:15) and He overcame them all and won the victory for us.

When in touch with the Lord daily we will realize that we have self worth and thereby respect for self and others and God for us, leaving us with a sense of fulfillment and purpose. Take Time to walk with Jesus and He will never leave your side. Remember, when God created you He didn't make a mistake.

Play

The American College Dictionary defines play as "to exercise or apply oneself in diversion, amusement, or recreation." This definition is provided for you so that we are on the "same page" in what we are about to share.

Many lives are confused and troubled simply because they don't have a healthy diversion. Jesus set the example for us when He would go to a mountain, a lake, or a friend's house, together with using every opportunity to worship in the Lord's house. Even when He faced His death, He went to the Garden of Gethsemane with those closest to Him to speak with His heavenly Father. We can learn from this not to take ourselves too seriously by working too hard and long for the sake of material comforts. Let us not confuse this "getting ahead" with one who must work to pay bills, but, even then, there needs to be a time to "rest" (and we don't mean sleep in bed).

Treasures in this writer's heart are the times spent with parents, family, and friends on Sunday afternoon or a weekday evening when we visited in our home. To play (as defined above) can happen in many ways: gardening, riding, sports, visiting, reading, going for a drive, taking a walk, jogging, bike riding, listening to your children, spouse, friend, etc. One is refreshed and invigorated by doing this, making ready for your daily routine. This holds true for those with the burdens with which they are faced day in and day out. Jesus knew what life was all about. Let us learn from Him and by Him. Let us learn to take time to be refreshed and find the secret of perpetual youth.

If you don't know where to begin there are various organizations and church groups in your community by which you can find something just right for you. If there should be nothing structured for you, why not get together with some friends of like interest and start a group that will provide you with a time to be refreshed through some God-pleasing activity?

Read

The Holy Bible says, "The fear of the Lord is the beginning of wisdom." (Psalm: 111:10). It would appear today that many do not read enough of God's Holy Word if we look at the degenerating morals of our nation right down to our local communities. Does one feel this because of getting older? No, not really! Plato, a Greek philosopher before Christ, spoke of the crumbling moral behavior of children in relationship to their parents. Now, let's go even farther back, to the time of Adam and Eve. One of their sons committed murder by killing his brother. Not too many generations later, all of civilization was destroyed by a great flood. There was a general moral rot among the people, with the exception of a father called Noah and his three sons. Together with their wives, they were spared because God and His way were honored. Again and again the people of old did it their way, ignoring God, and they suffered the result of their own ignorance.

Is there anything we can learn from history, Biblical or otherwise? Absolutely! Unless one reads and studies, he/she are committed to making the same mistake(s) over, never the wiser for it. This is a good time, generally speaking, for parents and children to begin reading not only the Holy Bible, but other acceptable material. The Bible says, "Study (God's own Holy Word) to show yourself approved unto God, rightly dividing the word of truth." (2 Timothy 2:15).

It is apparent to any honest observer that the hurt and pain in so many lives today could be averted had someone done some reading and searching to find answers that are pleasing to God for the vexing problems of today. The best Word to read for today is "Jesus." St. John the Gospel writer said, "In the beginning was the Word, and the Word was with God, and the Word was God...And the Word was made flesh and dwelt among us and we beheld His glory, the glory of the only begotten of the Father, full of grace and truth." (John 1:1,14)

The writer of Proverbs said: "Know that wisdom is sweet to your soul; if you find it, there is a future hope for you, and your hope will not be cut off." (Proverbs 24:14). In this new century, this new year, let us seek after wisdom, true wisdom, the wisdom of God in Jesus. Life will take on new meaning for you.

Laugh

Did you know that it takes fewer muscles in your face to laugh than it does for you to frown or scowl? Is this perhaps the great beauty aid which so many are searching for to rid their face of wrinkles?

The Bible says in Ecclesiastes 3:4 of laughter: "There is a time to weep and a time to laugh." The writer, in this chapter, speaks of just about everything in our lives and goes on to say "God has made everything beautiful in its time." (Ecclesiastes 3:11). Read this magnificent chapter about life. The beauty and innocence of God-fearing laughter is demonstrated by little children in their play and in their response to things around them as they enjoy living. We read in Genesis 21:6 about Sarah in her old age finding laughter in the gift of a child, and all around her laughed also in joy. In the Book of Job (56:22), we read the words "You will laugh at destruction and famine...." The victory belongs to the righteous, the God-fearing, as the psalmist says in Psalm 52:6: "The righteous will see and fear; they will laugh at him saying, 'Here now is the man who did not make God His stronghold....'"

Again and again we see from the Holy Word that laughter is a song of the human spirit to be enjoyed for good health and much happiness. We see a lot of worry wrinkles, but do not recall ever seeing someone with wrinkles from laughter. Perhaps God has made this truth simple enough for even the wise, as children, to understand the miracle of laughter as the key to the health of all people of all ages, of all walks of life. One cannot help but think that Jesus Himself enjoyed good, clean healthy laughter once in a while as

He carried out His ministry, perhaps when with children or with Martha, Mary, and Lazarus, His dear friends.

Let us all take some time to observe the simple things of life and enjoy to the point of laughter out of pure joy and happiness and the fact that God has done all things well in spite of man!

Memorial Day

We take some time to share some thoughts about a subject which causes fear, dread, and questions for many people, both young and old. We are celebrating Memorial Day with many of us decorating the graves of our loved ones who have gone before us. Our departed loved ones have already experienced our subject for this week and that subject is death.

It is safe to say that we fear death because no one we know here in this life has died and come back to tell us all about it. My friends, there is Someone Who can tell you all you need to know about this unpopular subject, one which we all face at some point. That someone is Jesus, who is both God and man and thereby qualified to speak.

First, Psalm 23:4 reads in the King James version of the Bible: "Yea, though I walk through the valley of the shadow of death, I will fear no evil, for Thou art with me." Here death is referred to as a shadow, and friend, a shadow cannot hurt you. He also says, "Thou art with me." We are never alone at the time of death. In John 14:3 Jesus says, when speaking to His disciples of why He must die, "I go to prepare a place for you and if I go to prepare a place for you, I will come again and take you unto myself, that where I am there you will be also.." Our family and friends can walk with us only to the doorway we call death, but Jesus waits at the doorway to walk with us into eternal life in Heaven where we shall be with Him always.

If you have questions and if you want to be sure of eternal life,

Jesus Christ is your Savior. Receive Him now by faith as your personal Savior and Companion, as God's free gift to you, a gift of the Holy Spirit. (Ephesians 2:8,9). When it comes your time to leave this life and that can be anytime (check the obituaries and look at the ages from the cradle to old age) be prepared. If Jesus Christ isn't your Savior and friend, then by God's grace and the power of the Holy Spirit, receive Him now. As Jesus said, "Whatsoever you shall ask the Father in my name, believing, you shall receive." Great peace awaits you on the other side. There is no need to fear death because it is a passage to be with Jesus.

Time-Off

We are all familiar with the term "time-off." It may or may not mean the same thing to all of us. For children, the phrase may be "time-out," as an exercise in behavior, whether as measure of correction, or to simply rest. For adults, perhaps both terms can be used, namely a "time-off" can be a "time-out." For this moment with you I will take both terms and use them interchangeably.

As we go about our daily lives whether young or old, healthy or not so, we all need to take a "time-out" to enjoy some "time-off." The perfect example before us is that of Jesus Himself, God's only Son, sent here among men to teach by word and example the way of a truly fulfilled life. In John 10:10 Jesus said "I have come that they may have life, and have it to the full." This helps us to understand and apply the words of John 14:6: "I am the Way, the Truth, and the Life...." This for the fullest understanding is our spiritual relationship with God first and second with each other.

As He fulfilled His purpose among men He took some "time-out" to refresh Himself with some "time-off." Jesus went out into the mountains to a quiet place to pray, to meditate, to be with His chosen disciples. He would spend time with Mary, Martha, and Lazarus, three special friends. Jesus attended a wedding at Cana and spared the host of the wedding some social embarrassment by performing His first miracle showing Who and What He was. Whie Jesus was dying on the cross, He took a brief moment to provide for the caring of His mother. Jesus spent time with children, with the sick, with the dying - all a part of His life.

Isn't it true that for the most part people work so hard at taking some "time-out" that when they are finished and back at work they feel tired but glad to be back in the routine and here they find their rest? I quote from At The Father's Table: "'The flowers appear on the earth; the time of the singing of birds is come' (song of Solomon 2:12). Are you one of those busy persons who can't take time ("time-off" or a "time-out) to see the flowers or listen to the birds sing? We pride ourselves on full schedules, involvement with work, and committee meetings. There is scarcely time to lift up our eyes to the hills or to walk beside the still water or smell the flowers. What a pity! But we can do that–if we want to.

Time is a sacred trust, which like all other gifts, has been entrusted to us as good stewards to be used wisely and properly with its "time-outs" and its "time-offs." We are to make good use of our time. (Psalm 90:12). There is a time for every purpose. (Ecclesiastes 3:1-8). All of our time is to be sanctified for good. (Ephesians 5:15-16). The greatest of all tragedies is when we delay that which belongs to peace with God. (Psalm 27:1). Why not be like the Lord, the Creator of Heaven and earth, and "rest" ("time-off)? "Take Time" to smell the roses, and you will be surprised at what you will discover.

Friendly

The holidays are past, and, for whatever reason, some are unhappy. Perhaps bills, lost friend, an emptiness within or an uncertain future has dampened the spirit. Much happens within our life which creates experiences in turn altering our mood. The ending of one century nearly five years ago and the beginning of another century has caused some to experience misgivings with events that surround their life today.

This is just the time when we need to reach out and be friendly with all around us. Friendly people are becoming fewer and fewer. For example, the lack of visiting one another in the home, not spending time with our family, being too busy to find out about the people we work with, and so the list goes on. In simple words, "Have we become too busy or self-centered?

The Lord Jesus Christ was never too busy for people, whether they were young or old, important or not important (that is, in the limelight or not), whether they were good citizens or rabble rousers. Granted, in today's society and culture there are those, if you look cross-eyed at them will have you in court faster than you can bat an eyelash. Is it that these among others are the cause of such distance between people? We have lost something that Jesus Christ taught.

When Jesus was asked what the greatest commandment of all was, He replied: "Love the Lord your God with all your heart and with all your soul, and with all your mind, and the second is like unto this, Love your neighbor as yourself." He did it, do we? Look around and you be the judge.

During this year and this century why not turn back the leaves of the pages of life to a time when people had time for each other, and most importantly, had time for God other than on the holy days of the year. Let God be in your life other than in the form of an expression as in "Oh my God," or, when you are sick, or when you die. We might all be surprised if God, the God of the Bible, took preeminence in the lives of all again. The change would be immediate in life around us. Make a belated resolution now: I will be friendly to all. What an easy road to happiness. Let us, as Jesus did and with Jesus in our heart, befriend all with whom we come into contact this day, this week, this month, this year and whenever. Let it begin with me this day.

Think

When we watch life happen around us, it makes us wonder if some even think when we see such senseless acts committed around us. The relationship of people with each other leaves much to be desired. While shopping, a young mother guiding three children through a busy store accidentally bumped, ever so slightly, another woman. The woman that was bumped said, "Excuse me!" And continued walking without a limp, complaining that she was really hurt by the "thoughtless" woman that bumped her. It makes one wonder if the young mother with the children was enjoying this "special" time with her children.

An old proverb says, "Think before you leap." Perhaps we would all do well to follow this advice. Would so many marriages fail if the couple had really gotten to know the other person's integrity and individuality? Would so many be unhappy at work if they took the time to know the person(s) with whom they work? Would we be so quick to judgement if we took the time to get to know all the facts before we spoke? Perhaps if we took the time to think about the beauty of life around us in the simple things, we would have less stress and conflict.

The Lord Jesus always took time to go off by Himself and pray and meditate (another way of looking at "thinking). He took time to consider His purpose, and He truly knew what that meant for His life. Jesus took time to sit with the children and listen. They can always make us think! The sick were always visited with compassion, which, if we did more of, would give us time to think about the blessings we have in our health. In our relationships we should follow the advice of another proverb: "Believe none of what you hear and half of what you see and question even that." Let thinking about the consequences of our actions always be foremost in our minds and hearts. Perhaps then it would be easier to follow the advice of the Word of God: "Love your neighbor as yourself," and "Whatsoever you would that men should do to you, do so unto them," and "Having food and clothing let us be content." If you want power (in the good sense) in your life take time to THINK before you leap. Wouldn't this be a great New Year's resolution to make and keep?

Christmas
Worship

This is the time of observing the holy day of Christ's birth despite the emphasis laid by men of our culture on materialism. The Child of God is being distracted by the "hype" of parties, shopping, and all else that has entered the picture. To be sure, these things are not wrong in and of themselves; but when they are abused, we lose the real meaning and purpose of Christmas.

Perhaps you have heard the story of two shoppers as Christmas was approaching. They came to a store front with the scene of the birth of Christ in a stable. One of the shoppers said "What do think of that? Now even the Christians are trying to get into Christmas." Somewhere, these shoppers "missed the boat." Whether one wants to admit it or not, the coming of the Savior, Jesus Christ, is what Christmas is all about. All the trimmings are only man-made attempts toward a festive spirit.

A good application of baking, decorations, gifts and gatherings can best be summed up in the words of a restaurant worker, who said, when asked why she was always smiling and laughing and speaking cheerful words: "Christmas is the time I find joy in getting a gift for someone and inviting them into my home and having a holiday meal with them as God did." Perhaps we should call this a contemporary application of the Gospel.

The God of the Bible tells as He speaks throughout the Holy Word that He finds only joy in giving the gift of His Son, Jesus Christ, and invites the whole world into His Home. He provides the meal of His life-giving Word out of love granting forgiveness, joy, and peace on earth. This alone makes for good will among men. All of this is yours by faith alone in Jesus Christ, God's Son, Who became flesh in the virgin Mary. He grew up to meet His heavenly Father's demands under His law, suffer and die and rise again. He is Who is coming again to claim His own. We sing

Joy to the world, the Lord is come,
Let earth receive her King.

In this spirit, why not go to a Christian church of worship and find the refreshing love of God? It is available for you and yours. Have a blessed Christmas with Christ, your Savior and Friend and Guide.

Lent

Trouble

Years ago a military officer and his wife were aboard a ship that was caught in a raging ocean storm. Seeing the frantic look in her eyes, the man tried unsuccessfully to allay her fears. Suddenly she grasped his sleeve and cried, "How can you be so calm?" He stepped back a few feet and drew his sword. Pointing at her heart, he said, "Are you afraid of this?" Without hesitation she answered, "Of course not!" "Why not?" He inquired. "Because it's in your hand, and you love me too much to hurt me." To this he replied, "I know the One who holds the winds and the waters in the hollow of His hand, and he will surely care for us!" The officer was not disturbed because he had put his trust in the Lord.

And so it is for us today in our lives, even when we find trouble which seems to have no end. Jesus said, "Don't let your hearts be troubled. Trust in God, and trust in Me." (John 14:1). Isaiah said in chapter 43:2, "When you pass through the water, I will be with you. When you cross rivers, you will not drown. When you walk through fire, you will not be burned, nor will the flames hurt you." St. Paul wrote in Romans 8: 29: "We know that in everything God works for the good of those who love Him." They are the people He called, because that was His plan. Psalm 121:1-2 says, "I look up to the hills, but where does my help come from? My help comes from the Lord, who made heaven and earth." St. Paul seems to sum it up when he says in Philippians 4:6-7, "Do not worry about anything, but pray and ask God for everything you need, always giving thanks. And God's peace, which is so great we cannot understand it, will keep your hearts and minds in Christ Jesus."

At times we are faced with seemingly insurmountable troubles which make life very painful. Remember this: God has not forgotten us nor forsaken us. He is right there beside us and will see us through. Job, in the Old Testament experienced this. David found this out when he was running and hiding for his life from King Saul. who planned to kill him. The woman in the gospels, who had an issue of blood for many years, came to Jesus in faith simply to touch the hem of His garment for she knew when would be healed. St. Paul came to Jesus with his "thorn in the flesh" (we don't understand what this was) relying on God's mercy and he, in faith, lived out his life seeing the Lord uncured. And so we can too! Cured or uncured, we can "do all through Christ, Who strengthens us." (Philippians 4:13). Give your trouble to the Lord and He will walk with you, enabling you to live.

During this Lenten season think on these things: Christ Jesus is our life and strength. Our life is in His hands, and like the military officer, let us put our trust in the Lord.

Spring

Weather

This is a good time to consider a few words on the most talked about subject between men and women. NO, IT IS NOT SEX! Rather it is the weather. Permit me to share with you a few words of verse written by John Ruskin: "Sunshine is delicious, rain is refreshing, wind braces up, snow is exhilarating, there is no such thing as bad weather, only different kinds of good weather." You know something, he is right. Only our perception, or mood(s), our emotions see rain, cloudiness, cold, and warmth as something negative for whatever weather.

We wish to share with you some thoughts from the Holy Scripture, which is God's gift to us and is without error, mistake, or contradiction. Only in the Holy Bible can we find something that makes sense. We will paraphrase by saying that rain, sunshine, summer, winter, cold, warmth, seedtime and harvest will always be for our benefit. The problem for many is that they want it their way. God has never made a mistake or failed us yet! We may have less one year and more another, but we shall never be without the necessities of life. God said, "Having food and clothing, let us be content." (1 Timothy 6:8). In the Lord's Prayer Jesus taught us, "Give us this day our daily bread" to be fulfilled in what we have as we do our best and as we are given as a wage that provides us with that which we need to live contentedly every day.

God, by means of the weather, gives us such beauty and satisfaction if we take the time to notice His love for us. Did you notice this Spring the beauty in the color of hues of the budding trees and shrubs and now the beautiful colors of green which appear so rich in all their splendor? Every time we see a seed's sprout break through the soil and watch it break out with such incredible beauty, it is a miracle for us to see. Let this invitation be yours: put down the newspaper, the stock report, turn off the TV and radio, hang up the phone and put the cell phone away (turn it off), attend a little league ball game, go out for a quiet walk or drive and observe God's beauty given us. Leave the meeting you were to attend after a long day at work and spend some time with family and friends (in that order) by going to a park, or, just sit out in your yard and listen to God surround you with His love in the soft sound of rain falling, the rustling of leaves, the singing of birds, or, just see in the beauty of all of God's creatures which sing their little hearts out.

This writer would be remiss if it was not said that primary to all is that you would take Jesus, Who is in charge of all, and spend some quiet time with that One Who gives us the strength to do all things in the first place. St. Paul said, "I can do all things through Christ Who strengthens me." (Philippians 4:13). For my life would be impossible without Him to give me an understanding of what is happening in any form in all that surrounds me, especially with the weather. It is with the touch of the Master's hand that we can be at peace with the weather and all that happens around me.

The Guide

Today, in the newspapers, on television, in all ways of communication, we have put before us guides to living. And yet, crime increases. There is more abuse of every sort; disrespect is shown in all areas of living; there is more hostility, and less and less peace and love among people. What is one to do?

First, let it be said that the Holy Bible is God speaking to us today and not to another generation. Sad to say, even some Christian churches say that the Bible is to be taken in the light of its context of another time period and therefore it is not all there is to say about life (both before God and man) today. This could not be farther from the truth. The Holy Bible is just as true today as when God inspired man to write it. It is without error and totally correct in all its parts. The Holy Bible is completely dependable, and we can go to it for seeing God's Way of salvation and the only Way to live before God and with man. It is the only source of living for today as we shall find in a true search for life and meaning.

Second, the Bible is God-given. "Holy men of God spoke as they were moved by the Holy Ghost." (2 Peter 1:21). The Bible is God's power for our salvation as we read in Romans 1:16: "I am not ashamed of the Gospel of Christ, for it is the power of God unto salvation to every one that believes...." The Bible, God's Holy Word, is the only way for the new birth: "Being born again, not of corruptible seed, but of incorruptible, by the Word of God which liveth and abideth forever." (1 Peter 1:23). The Word of God is for every day of life: "Thy Word is a lamp unto my feet, and a light unto my path." (Psalm 119:105). The Bible records the love of

God for all: "For God so loved the world, that He gave His only begotten Son, that whosoever believeth in Him should not perish, but have everlasting life." (John 3:16).

Third, let us leave the Word of God as it was given and not submit it to our own private interpretation to do whatsoever we want. Rather, let us turn to it in all areas of our life: spiritual, religious, emotional, and physical. Let it stand as God intended it and not make it fit our own selfish lifestyle of this century. In it we can find hope, peace, love, joy, strength, and life for both now and hereafter. Let God speak for Himself and let God in His Word be your Guide.

Rain

Rain is one of the most commonly talked about subjects in the life of all people, young and old. Songs have been sung about it and books of every nature have been written about it in man's quest to understand the life that surrounds him. Professions have developed around it for the benefit of all. When one thinks about the comments made about rain one is grateful that one is not God because who among men could withstand the comments of others. For humans, there is either too much or too little, it should have been yesterday, or, it could have waited until tomorrow. The rain came down too hard or, the mist (meaning it should have rained harder) wasn't enough to make a difference. And so it goes on and on.

Thank God, He is in charge! He treats all alike, or equal, as the Bible says, "He sends rain on the just and on the unjust." If man were in charge, he would have a bias, but not so with God. We can learn much from this necessity of life without which we would all die (although little children might disagree when it comes to bath time). In the years of life which the Lord has blest us with, God has never yet failed us and He never will. We need to look more to God and His perspective the next time we wish to complain about too much or too little, or, the wrong time. Usually our complaints come out of selfish motivation. God's actions come out of love.

Some of the blessings of life with regard to rain, are the food we eat, the clothes we wear, the beauty that surrounds us in nature with its bounty of blessings from its seemingly limitless supply and variety of flowers, plants, and trees. The rain is always there for us in the production of food, if not where we live, then, where someone else lives, and we or they supply the other with our daily need. Not only did God create us, but He still preserves us with all that we need to support this body and life. What a marvelous, caring, loving and thoughtful God we have that watches over us. We need to count all our blessings, among which is the rain. Thank you, Lord.

Trim

People who work in the yard are familiar with trimming. Bushes, shrubs, and trees are trimmed that they might produce more, look better, or just add to the general beauty of the yard. It never ceases to amaze me when I buy a new shrub. The directions say that if the shrub is not already trimmed back, I am to do so before planting. When it then grows, it grows so full and rich with its beauty. Life is much like this.

Trimming is nothing new. The Lord spoke of trimming a tree or vine that did not produce, and even when producing, it was to be trimmed back still more that it might produce more. There is a lesson here for all people to learn. At times in our lives we experience some kind of hardship in one form or another. At the time it hurt so terribly that we could not find the words to describe what it was doing to us. When it was past, we could look back and see what the Lord was trying to teach us. We do not always have the answers, at least for the moment, but a time comes, or will come, when we do have the answer. St. Paul said, "Now we see through a glass darkly, but then, face to face." In other words, the time comes when we shall have the answer(s) we desire now, but to have them now is not always necessary. We do survive without them.

The next time you are experiencing pain of one sort or another, try to picture the Master Gardener working with you that your life might be richer and fuller. We might not always understand at the moment, but the time comes when we shall. That's the beauty of living. As the writer of Ecclesiastes said, (chapter 3) "God has made everything beautiful in its time." Read this chapter of God's Holy Word and much light can be shed on everyday experiences that add meaning and richness to living.

Hurt

All people experience "hurt" at one time or another in their life. Children experience all kinds of "hurt," namely their bodies, whether real or imagined, their minds and emotional composure again for various reasons. Adults are "hurt" by broken promises or ill spoken words, or angry deeds done against them. No one is exempt from the pain of "hurt." All age groups experience "hurt" in their lives at one time or another.

Perhaps the worst kind of hurt is the hurt caused by a friend, one we trust, one in whom we place our all and they turn on us and for whatever reason they believe they have, they hurt us badly by what they say about us or do to us. Some of this hurt can never be corrected. It can be endured; it can be forgiven, but never undone.

Our Lord was no different in this experience with others either. He has set before us an example of what to do with those who hurt us, namely, forgive them and love them in spite of themselves or the hurt endured. Jesus was hurt by the politicians, the military, His own race, the religious leaders and teachers of His day, and His own friends. His first words from the cross were "Father, forgive them...," not "Get me a lawyer." He spoke kindly to those who came to Him for understanding and help and ear to listen. We can be no less than this for all those near and dear to us.

This is what the body of Christ is all about. When we hurt, the rest are here for lifting us up or at least helping us carry our burden. Thank God for the Christian family. We need to listen more regularly to the words of Christ the Lord not only when we hurt, but also when all is well. Then, life is always as beautiful as Spring with its flowers, and changing colors, and fresh showers and bright sun, for as Jesus said, "I am come that they might have life and have it overflowing."

Thoughtfulness

There are many occasions in our lives that bring acts of some kindness and love, some thoughtfulness and concern by someone special in our lives which make living more appreciated. Birthdays, anniversaries, a job well done, or, simply being a part of the family or community that says thank you in some meaningful way for what we have done means so very much.

Perhaps the saddest experience is to have some one take from us and not say thank you. Parents are often not thanked for their many sacrifices and gifts which include education, a special request that is in vogue, and the like. Husbands and wives after a while take each other for granted and forget the little things that once were done but now because of familiarity, life is left to go its own way and each forget to express their love and appreciation, and a distance grows between them.

It seems that many individuals, whether in families or in larger communities, take for granted the other's contribution to their life and happiness. Soon strife of one kind or another follows and so unhappiness and grief enter the picture of our daily existence. What one word of kindness would do if it were only spoken!

Christ Jesus often acted in such a way that those close to Him and even strangers never needed to guess about His thoughtfulness and kindness and unique concern for them. It was so evident in the little things He did among them. Jesus was true man and experienced all that we are tested with and yet He overcame those trials without sinning, thus, giving us the power to live because we know that someone truly does care about us each and every day of our lives. (Psalm 139 fulfilled). How precious is His love and thoughtfulness for us and all others because we are members of His family. Lest us live the same way with each other and make this day a little brighter. " I can do all things through Christ Who strengthens me," so said St. Paul. Try saying "Thank you" with a word or a smile, or do some deed of kindness, or give someone a hug and see how much the world changes around you - not only for others abut also for yourself!

Post Easter/Spring

Spring/Life

Spring produces many images in our minds, but specifically the most beautiful image that come to mind is all that is brought forward, that is new and renewed. We have new life in flowers, plants, shrubs, trees, birds and animals of all kinds, the crops in the fields, and the weather changes that take place. For a few people, spring is a factor in their health that is very depressing; however, for most people it is the opposite. Spring is life and joy and hope and all that excites people and makes them forget many sad experiences of life.

For Christians, spring is also the time of celebration of another kind of life that proclaims "Christ is risen!", the message which many celebrated a few weeks ago with enthusiasm because it was the celebration of life over death. God has done all possible for us to learn the wonderful story of life. He has given us reminders of life in almost all things. In spring people head for the gardens with "gusto" and plant all types of seeds and plants with anticipation of life in the plants they envision as growing in their little gardens. However, with that planting comes the responsibility of caring and nurturing. For some, the anticipation soon turns to drudgery over the work involved and these folks would not hesitate to let someone else do the work of caring for that garden life.

Similarly, but sadly so, there is the likeness with regard to human life. A new baby, for example, at first almost always invokes great joy, but then come the sleepless nights, the illnesses that keep the care givers up and busy, and all the little things that go into the loving and raising of that baby to a child and then teenager and an adult. And sadly enough, some leave this part of life in the hands of others. Why can't all people learn the simple beauties of life in the giving and caring for that life and thereby enjoy the greatest gift of all?

There is a need to turn to the Lord Jesus and learn of the gift of life, which He has won for us and gives to us through the simplest of means, namely, faith, that which trusts Him completely, and receive freely the gift of life. Let spring and this time after the magnificent celebration of the resurrection of Jesus Christ be a time of celebration and humble acceptance of all that goes with the responsibility of caring for life itself. Let us all learn what life is truly about from the greatest example of all, Jesus Christ.

Post Easter/Spring
Spring/Life

Spring produces many images in our minds, but specifically the most beautiful image that come to mind is al that is brought forward that is new and renewed. We have new life in flowers, plants, shrubs, trees, birds and animals of all kinds, the crops in the fields, and the wether changes that take place. For a few people, Spring is a factor in their health that is very depressing; however, for most people it is the opposite. Spring is life and joy and hope and all that excites people and makes them forget many sad experiences of life.

For Christians, Spring is also the time of celebration of another kind of life that proclaims "Christ is risen!", the message which many celebrated a few weeks ago with enthusiasm because it was the celebration of life over death. God has done all possible for us to learn the wonderful story of life. He has given us reminders of life in almost all things. In Spring people head for the gardens with "gusto" and plant all types of seeds and plants with anticipation of life in the plants they envision as growing in their little gardens. However, with that planting comes the responsibility of caring and nurturing. For some the anticipation soon turns to drudgery over the work involved, and these folks would not hesitate to let someone else do the work of caring for that garden life.

Similarly, but sadly so, there is the likeness with regard to human life. A new baby, for example, at first almost always invokes great joy, but then come the sleepless nights, the illnesses that keep the care givers up and busy, and all the little things that go into the loving and raising of that baby to a child and then teenager and an adult. And sadly enough, some leave this part of life in the hands of others. Why can't all people learn the simple beauties of life in the giving and caring for that life and thereby enjoy the greatest gift of all?

There is a need to turn to the Lord Jesus and learn of the gift of life, which He has won for us and gives to us through the simplest of means, namely, faith, that which trusts Him completely, and receive freely the gift of life. Let Spring and this time after the magnificent celebration of the resurrection of Jesus Christ be a time of celebration and humble acceptance of all that goes with the responsibility of caring for life itself. Let us all learn what life is truly about from the greatest example of all, Jesus Christ.

The Lowly Sparrow

We so often rush that which is "commonplace" in life and thereby it is often ignored or lost. We learn much about the art of living by watching the little things of life that surround us. One of the most interesting of these is the lowly sparrow. This little bird, a foreigner to this land until brought here by the early settlers, has adapted itself and is content where it lives. Like people, the sparrow "needs its space," a phrase common to our lives today. When it eats, sleeps, or sits on a fence just watching life go by, it is always near its neighbor, always there to warn its neighbor if an enemy is close at hand; always there to support the group "chorus" with its loud chatting. The sparrow never worries about what it shall eat or where it shall sleep.

Our heavenly Father calls our attention to the sparrow in the gospel of Matthew (10:29) where Matthew writes that the sparrow does not fall to the ground without the Father's knowledge. The heavenly Father keeps track of each one without exception. Man, however, values the sparrow so little.

Perhaps we can learn a lesson here. We are so bothered with each day's affairs that we worry ourselves near to death when all along the heavenly Father is in charge and always will be. To make sure, we all need to use our talents and gifts from the heavenly Father and not expect others to do it for us. Like the lowly sparrow, we must be concerned for those around us, stay near to those about whom we have a great concern, and always trust the heavenly Father for His loving care and protection for all.

As children of the heavenly Father in Christ Jesus our Lord, we can always rest assured that our lives, our needs, our concerns, our hurts, our family, and all else that is of concern to us is under the watchful eye of the heavenly Father. Trust Him! Take Time to learn from the lowly sparrow.

Relationships

Were it only possible for there to be peace in the world, in our nation, our state, our community, our homes, and in our lives. So much is disturbing in what surrounds us. Today on the news we heard that in the southern part of Africa one of two young people have AIDS; in the U.S. the Supreme Court struck down, in one state (there are 22 other states with a similar law), a law that protected the human life from late term abortions; more than half of all marriages end in divorce; more and more children are being raised with one parent; drugs among high school youth is on the increase; the rate of people living together outside of marriage is rising; a TV show on ABC has turned Jesus Christ, God's Son, from Savior into just another reactionary, the Holy Scriptures into just another book that cannot be trusted and so the list could go on. The point is made that a God-fearing relationship is no longer "cool."

What can be said of all this? St. Matthew has said it well in his words of the Gospel of Matthew, chapter 15, verses 19 and 20: "For out of the heart come evil thoughts, murder, sexual immorality, theft, false testimony, slander. These are what make a man 'unclean:'...." All of these we recognize around us today. Where can we find any hope? Any peace? Any comfort? The Psalmist said: "God, your love is so precious! You protect people in the shadow of your wings." (Psalm 36:7). Again: "Those who go to God Most High for safety will be protected by the Almighty. I will say to the Lord, 'You are my place of safety and protection. You are my God and I trust you.' God will save you from hidden traps and from deadly diseases." (Psalm 91:1-3).

The answer to a world running "amuck" is found at the feet of God and cross of His Son, Jesus Christ. This is a beautiful world and all that God created is beautiful. Just look around you at His creation. For anything to change in our relationship(s), it needs to begin with you and me living in the footsteps of the God/Man, Jesus Christ. It is sung in a song: "Let there be peace on earth and let it begin with ne." Let all slow down in life and live in the shadow of the Lord. Here there is comfort for all who would ask of the Lord, for all who would walk in His way. Let us regain the values of bygone days and live them with all whom we love under the guidance of Almighty God. Herein lies the basis of true and lasting relationships of friendship, of strong homes, of lasting marriages, of hearts and minds that are filled with true and lasting love that gives itself for each other because it has already started with the Lord Jesus Christ. With Him you have the foundation for lasting relationships.

Holy Week
Crowns of Thorns and Glory

From shame to honor, from tragedy to triumph, from suffering and death to resurrection and new life - - this was the mission of our blessed Lord Jesus. This too is the path of life we must tread on this earth if we are to be His faithful disciples.

In this Lenten season and especially during this Holy Week, we are to remember gratefully the sacrifice of Jesus, the spiritual and physical pain and anguish He suffered. Thus, he identified Himself with us in His humanity. In His Deity, He would be raised again from the dead and be our risen and glorified Lord.

This is depicted with real insight with "Good" Friday's crown of thorns which, on that day, Jesus made into blossoms of glory and great beauty. The Crown of Life is above the cross and so the Christian can truly say, "in the cross of Christ I glory, towering o'er the wrecks of time," because it is the glad, grateful song of the redeemed of all time.

We shall always remember what our dear Lord bore for us. We shall also be grateful that He burst asunder the bonds of death on Easter morning, and we shall all cry with the whole Church around the world, "Alleluia! Christ is risen!"

You are invited to worship in a Christian church of your choice on this special morning which believing truly in the bodily resurrection of Jesus Christ our living Lord, join Christians from around the world in this great and glorious celebration. What a victory is ours over our greatest enemies of sin, death, and the devil! "Christ is Risen!" "He is risen indeed!"

Responsibility

At various times much is said about the acceptance of responsibility in private life. For example, as we live in our community (education, morals, city clean-up, life in the community), and in our state and nation and the world. It all comes down to the individual; and isn't it time everyone accepts moral, ethical and spiritual responsibility and end the looking to "the other person" to provide?

Some want to live with the philosophy that "everybody owes them a living" and they really don't care what happens. And then, there are those who won't accept responsibility for any moral behavior whatever, except to do what they want without any concern for what happens in and to themselves and their community. For some, the responsibility of education in the home, the state, and the nation is turned over to the "authority," whomever that might be. In simple terms, do what you want and condemn everyone else for the problems in one's own life. This is seen in the "political" pundits in our life today.

There once was a young man who took his inheritance and went out and lived without answering to anyone, because in his mind what was yours was his and what was his was his. After his inheritance was all gone along with his friends, there was only one place to which he could turn and that was to the home of his father. In his circumstance he was ready to work as a servant. However, the father kept his responsibility and received his son back in full forgiveness out of love.

We are responsible for our actions. We are responsible to ourselves, to our family, to our neighbor, to our friends, to our community, to the state, to the nation, and to the world, but most important of all, to God. We are to live as "children of the heavenly Father." This means living with the responsibility of everything sacred to that family, namely,, the family of God. Doing so will reflect in our daily lives and all our relationships. God paid for you and redeemed you, adopted you in His Son Jesus Christ that you might have life and have it abundantly in its truest and most God-fearing responsibility. This is responsible living with responsible action in its truest form. To this we have all been called. And this responsibility for us is to live as sons and daughters of the Father and not as immoral, irresponsible "spiritual pigs" doing as we please, wallowing in whatever "hole of abject spiritual poverty" we can find.

Live with Christ in His way, and you will find the greatest sense of responsibility and the purest sense of fulfillment you have ever dreamed possible. Remember the "Golden Rule": "Do unto others as you would have them do unto you." Take Time and it just might work.

Easter

Easter Lives

The festival of Easter is past with many happy memories and thoughts we treasure. Memories of family or friends getting together for a joyous time of celebration. Memories of times past for some. Sighs of relief for those who made a lot of preparations and were worn out from them. We could list much more as we think of the festival now past.

BUT, there is more to Easter than the gatherings of dinners and breakfasts, and Easter egg hunts. Sometimes we get so busy trying our hand at living that we miss so much of the real beauty of God's love which is the real reason Christians celebrate Easter. Namely, Christ Jesus came; He saw; and He conquered the three arch enemies of us all: sin, death, and the devil. What a victory was His and ours through Him today. Living with Christ in your heart and in your life is really living.

Here is where memories of Easter past and the experience of Easter present really live for us. We remember and see the filled churches, the joyous singing of words proclaiming the greatest joy and comfort for all, the inspired messages, the faith proclaimed and not denied! So much in our lives today leaves one with fear and emptiness. BUT NOT CHRIST, the Lord! Christ has defeated death and has brought life and immortality to light for each of us. Some say to prove that He rose, but, in return let them prove He didn't rise from the dead. Here is where God's people find their strength for living through the daily experiences of life. Here is where strength waits for you with the living Lord and Christ Who has conquered all.

When Christian communities give testimony of a Lord Who cares so much that He won the victory for all and that community shares that truth with all, we are bound to see a difference. Easter lives because Christ lives and the message in our heart carries us on despite the challenges in our daily lives which would want us to believe something else to the contrary. The heart of Easter, Jesus Christ, truly lives today and shall never die. This year let us all take time to fill the Christian houses of worship and rejoice because Christ is risen!

Post Easter
Routine

Now the major festivals of the Christian year are concluded, at least as far as many are concerned. So where do we go from here? We pray that most, if not all, celebrated in the cycle of Christmas, Lent, and Easter the real reason for celebration, namely the coming of the Christ "in the fullness of time" when God "sent forth His Son, made of a woman, made under the Law, to redeem them under the Law that we might receive the adoption as sons (and daughters)." That Jesus did and now rules all things as the Victor, the Conqueror, the King Who lives and shall never again have to suffer such humiliation and pain and loneliness. Neither shall we. We are more than conquerors of all things that affect our lives through Christ the Lord.

In our daily lives we can so easily slip into a routine in which we take so much for granted. We take one another for granted, we take daily food for granted, we take our health for granted, we take our Savior for granted by the routines we develop which never really give us a chance to celebrate with deep conviction the great victory of Jesus Christ. "He has risen" takes on a "so what" attitude. May the Holy Spirit move our hearts in such a way that we never, when it comes to Christ Jesus in our lives, let Him slip from number one spot in our whole being.

If you are lonely, feeling forsaken, experiencing distress, or just plain down, remember the great love God has for you as He demonstrated in His Son Jesus Christ. Routine will never again rule your life for in Him each day will be new and exciting no matter what may befall you and yours. Celebrate each day, as at Easter, with faithful vigor and trust in Christ Jesus, the Lord of all life.

Holy Week
Living

What does really living mean to you? A good house to live in? A comfortable bank account? A goodly number of friends? A place of honor in your community? When a survivor at a grave side saw the deceased being buried in a Cadillac, he was overheard to remark: "Now that's really living!" Somehow when we hear something like that, we get the feeling that some priorities are mixed up, to say the least.

It was no different in Jesus' time. People were looking for an earthly king, when Jesus came. He was heard to say to the throngs of people that followed Him, that His purpose was not to be an earthly king. People left Him by throngs as well. On the night before His death He met only with His twelve disciples of whom even one of them betrayed Him.

Who or what is Jesus to you? He came that we might have life and have it abundantly. (John 10). He said that we were to take up our cross and follow Him. (Mark 8). His way was, as is ours, the way of denial of self (Matthew 16). In the eyes of the world and many around us, these statements are words of failure. According to them, one wouldn't say that you were really living.

WRONG! This Holy Week we once again focus very personally on the real "living" that is there for all. Christ is very personal, and Christ is very real. He wants all to know this. On Thursday evening many Christians will celebrate the Lord's Supper, commonly referred to as the "Last Supper" of Jesus. We have this New Covenant with God and from God, in which He renews His personal words of kinship and living with and for all. On Good Friday we gather together to we commemorate His death on the cross for all those things we fail in doing by thought, word, and deed. We enter into a time of reflection upon our "living" and bring it into compliance with that of the Lord Jesus Christ.

AND THEN ON EASTER MORNING WE CELEBRATE THE GREATEST VICTORY EVER IN THE HISTORY OF MAN! There are some who have great difficulty speaking of death, but what they fail to see is that beyond death (because of Christ's "living") is life for all who would have it for themselves. This life is in Christ Jesus the Lord and is yours simply by believing it! Humbly accept that truth in faith without any reservation or doubt. With Christ Jesus the Living Lord, you can really live. My friend, go to a truly Christian Church that knows Christ personally and celebrate what Jesus calls really "living." In Christ there is no loss, no defeat, no end, BUT ONLY LIVING. Take Time to worship with your spiritual brothers and sisters that One Who rules in life this day.

Quiet Time

In this "modern" age in which we live "Quiet Time" is a lost art for most people in their daily lives. "Busy" is the order of the day and night. Some don't really know why, but they keep busy all the same; and when the day is over, they cannot recall what they have done of value.

Jesus has something to say. When He finished preaching, healing, or, just being with people, He would go off by Himself. This was His "quiet time." We know of Gethsemane; we know of the mountains; and we know of His going to the temple. In each instance, He sought to be alone for "quiet time." In each instance, read that He was refreshed and strengthened.

In some instances Jesus would take His disciples along. It meant much to Him that those whom He loved were with Him to share in those "quiet times" as He so taught them.

Today, we need to understand that it is healthy to have some "quiet time" for ourselves. We need a time when we can talk with God, when we can meditate or think about life around us and our part in it and what we are doing about it. We can read the Sacred Scriptures which, it appears today, is a lost art among us, much less reading anything of value from other sources. The Bible says, "As a man thinks in His heart, so is he." This means knowing who and what we are. If we don't take time for ourselves, we will never know, will we? We will only be what we hear others say of us, and most frequently what we hear from others is not good. If we listen to the Lord, Who truly loves us so dearly, it is He that truly counts and none other. When we have listened to Him, then we will better know ourselves. This takes "quiet time." You can spend this time walking, sitting and listening to life around you (and not in front of the TV), gardening, golfing, fishing, being with your family and so on. Make your "quiet time" count! Spend it with the Lord and yourself, and you will be the better for it.

Trust

Trust is important to each of us regardless of age or position. When children have that trust betrayed by those they love, they are often hurt for life and are forever changed. When a confidence is broken by a friend, that friendship will never be the same. When the husband/wife relationship is betrayed, that union is forever affected. We need to trust our family, our doctor, our teachers, our co-workers, our neighbors, our government, and ourselves; or life will be a continuous experience of fear and anxiety and unhappiness.

The Lord offered simple but powerful advice for the lives of all His people everywhere. That advice begins first with trusting the Lord with all our heart, mind, and soul. This is the foundation of trust in all relationships. If we supplant God in our lives with something or someone else, that basis is lost.

Many people today attempt to live lives without the Lord for whatever reason they have conjured up in their minds, real or otherwise. It can't be done! It's as simple as that. God is trustworthy and He is dependable. He is always there for us. He has paid the greatest price so that our life will have purpose and meaning in the giving of His only Son. With Christ at the heart of all our behavior - thought, word, and deed - you cannot lose because He has never gone back on His Word and He never will! He has never given us reason to not trust Him.!

There is an old commercial which says, "Trust the man who wears the star." Rather, let us say "trust the Man Who carried the cross."

I sincerely hope that you will take some advice, if you haven't already, namely, trust Him with all your heart to do it best when we do it His way. Your life will have the greater peace and fulfillment than you can ever imagine possible. Try it, you might like it.

Life With Meaning

Just why do we exist here in this life anyway? We hear of and see pain and suffering all around us. There is so much of which we do not understand and so little we have control over. The same is true for all ages. Working with people brings us into contact with many "direction-less" men and women, young and old. There are days when people just want to give up.

It is certain one cannot live for material things to have meaning. The young man in the Biblical story of the Prodigal Son should show us that if we live only for the day and live only for "things," we will end up all alone and groveling in the pit of anxiety and despair. There has to be more to living than only the hedonistic approach of "eat, drink, and be merry for tomorrow we may die" approach to life which we see happening all around us.

First, we need to know that we are someone special and not just animal. God created man in His image which man lost through his disobedience and God restored through the promise of life and the sending of His Son Jesus Christ and which is ours through faith in this Jesus Christ as the One that counts in our life. In Jesus we all have a meaning and purpose beyond this life, a concept which the world and those without Christ cannot understand.

Second, we have one Who loves us for the person we are and Who gives us the strength to go beyond ourselves and to find meaning and purpose. Within that being we are which God has created and in whom He has a personal and meaningful interest. (Read Psalm 139).

Third, we must live for a reason: the use of each gift God has given us. Life is more than self-centered indulgence. When life has direction, there is very little that can destroy who and what we are by virtue of the God Who cares for and loves us. The wayward son found that demonstrated by his father when he came home and was welcomed back into the family circle. There is always a place for us with the Lord Himself.

Fourth, we must be determined with positive guides (Holy Scripture and common sense) to live our lives with integrity and purpose and with meaning. Here is truly meaningful living. Take Time to find peace with God and within yourself in this life through faith in Jesus Christ Who is truly "the Way, the Truth, and the Life" (John 14:6a) as your Savior and you shall find that life does have beautiful meaning. Your are somebody important to your Lord and for yourself.

Evening

Our lives are filled with beautiful experiences, events, and people. All go into that which builds our lives. One of the most beautiful experiences we have is to relax and reflect upon what has gone before us, what has happened with the people that we have met in the hours just behind us. One such time is in the evening when we can sit down and pause for a moment to count our blessings.

A good time for reflection and enjoyment is the evening when all begins to dim and grow dark and all nature sings its choruses of praise to God as the Psalmist says. There is nothing more beautiful than the evening sunset with birds singing together with the insects, "All is well, God is good!"

One of our troubles today is the fast pace of living in which we find ourselves. We haven't the time to even think of these special times. When was the last time you sat down and looked up into the darkening blue sky? It is so beautiful to see a cloud or two moving across and disappearing from the sky with the trail of a Jet or two with all of their passengers with their thoughts, conversations flying somewhere for whatever reason. Along with this beauty the chimney sweeps and nighthawks are chattering away chasing after their last meal for the day. Then we can sing with them "All is well, God is good!"

In times as these we need to get away for a few moments to reflect upon the past few hours of our lives to see that not all is or has been bad and that God is still in control regardless of man made events. It is of great interest to me that God, in the first book of the

Bible, Genesis, and in the first chapter, six times reflected upon that day's events and said, "It is good!" Can we not learn this from Him Who created all? If He had time for reflection, should we not also?

If your life is hectic and distressing and leaves you stressed out, stop for a moment in the evening to simply enjoy the purest of all pleasures, God's creation itself. That's why evening is so beautiful and serene and comforting and pure for the people of God even if things have gone badly. Truly, this is the pause that refreshes. Take a moment to walk with God in some quiet time for yourself. With the Psalmist let us too say: "Oh, give thanks unto the Lord, for He is good and His mercy endures forever."

Sunrise

Each day has a beauty all its own. Some favor the time of sunrise, others the day itself, and still others the sunset time of the 24 hours we have marked for the passing of time.

The expressions of the day are used by some to mark the span of human life, others the making of history. Whatever your familiarity with these expressions, my favorite time of day is sunrise, no, it is sunset. It's hard to pick a favorite time because each is special, isn't it? Sunrise, however, is the bright awakening to a new day with the hope of better things to come for each of us. There is a spirit of freshness and brightness to the ending of darkness during which many people experience a form of pain which sunrise drives away.

We see in sunrise a spirit of hope. We are urged with a determination to work harder for a better day than the one before. We have a whole new day before us of which we live only one second, one minute, one hour at a time as a gift to enjoy from God Himself. It is sad when one abuses the day and hurts another or even themselves in this precious time allotted.

Each sunrise is a gift from God to use for His glory and the good of our family, our neighbors (community), ourselves. When we fail to recognize this gift from God, we fail to know of a caring God Who moves in time and Who grants us forgiveness and another opportunity to make right, to improve, to rejoice and to give thanks in serving God, others, and then ourselves.

We need to take the time God gives us and enjoy even the smallest of beauties like a hummingbird feeding in the flowers, a wren singing a cheerful song, and all the magnificent sounds surrounding a people alive taking care of all which God has entrusted to them. Our Lord would invite us to see in the sunrise the beginning of a new day of hope and love and trust in God, Who alone has the power over all things. Let us commit the sunrise and all the time God allots to each of us to slow down and enjoy all that lies ahead of us and so have a good day. Let us remember, sunrise is a gift from God in which He lays before us a whole panorama of beauty which far surpasses the things which we may not understand and which may hurt us for only a short while. The brightness of a new day says God loves us.

Friends

From the earliest age, "friends" have been very basic. From the little children to the very elderly, we depend a great deal upon our friends for support, understanding, encouragement, and all else that brings peace and happiness in life. We all need a friend, one to whom we can turn, to confide in and trust.

The Holy Bible says a great deal about friends. "Greater love has no man than this that a man lay down his life for his friends." (John 15:13). This is the greatest of what we know as sacrifice; yet, people are ready to do just that for their friends. In the Bible we have the great example of two very good friends in the persons of David and Jonathan. When David's life was in jeopardy, Jonathan, his true friend and with the danger of sacrificing his life if caught, remained faithful to David as his friend and provided for the safety of the future king.

We need a great deal of this type of devotion today. Focus seems to be shifting from our friends to ourselves for many people, and in these instances "friends" are there for the single purpose of meeting our needs and our own ends. How could we have come so far in such an extreme change? Perhaps it is because the greatest friend one has ever had has become lost in many people's lives. This friend being spoken of is Jesus. We sing of this truth in a beautiful hymn:

What a friend we have in Jesus, All our sins and grief to bear!
What a privilege to carry   Everything to God in prayer!
Oh, what peace we often forfeit, Oh, what needless pain we bear,

All because we do not carry everything to God in prayer!

This friend Jesus is always there for us, and we can always talk with Him about anything in life because He was, as Scripture says, "tested in everything" and overcame all. He did it perfectly for us, His friends. What a Friend you have in Jesus!

Company

For the most part we all like to have company come to our home for a visit. All too often such visits are few and far between for whatever reason we think we may have. When someone does come there is a lot of "ketchin' up" to do with family news and any other news of importance.

Indirectly we are all company or visitors to this beautiful creation of God's. Sad to say His creation is not treated with love and respect by all and at times some of His special creations called "people" are not treated with love and respect either. Some of this "special creation" called "man" is misused and abused by the social "bullies" and special interest groups that are in this life to get from it what they can to advance themselves and their own causes regardless of the cost to someone else.

Christ Jesus came among men as God's chosen Way for peace in its most beautiful form. The Bible says a great deal about loving our neighbor as ourselves. (Read Matthew 5) Maybe this explains why some people have such a difficult time in getting along with their neighbor: they don't love themselves and don't know how to love their neighbor. The Bible says that we are to make the most of our time "while it is day before the night comes when no can work."

There is a little thing we often do with the word JOY. In describing our relationship with others, "J" means Jesus first, "O" means others second, and "Y" means yourself last. When we approach life in such a manner, indeed "company" takes on such a rich and full meaning when all is put in perspective. We can enjoy each other's company because of the contributions each can make. We can be blest with all of God's creation if we remember we are visitors (company) here on earth and all of His majesty is displayed for our enjoyment. Let us take the time to enjoy the time we have with each other and all blessings in whatever form they may take. Let us live each day to its fullest in a God-pleasing manner. Give the best of yourself and you will find it's returned a hundredfold. God bless you! Enjoy your company and be good company.

Fruits of Life

You have heard it said that "you get from life what you put into it." There is some truth here, but not always. Let us look at what we do get from life. It is harvest time and for gardeners, "harvest-time" has been going on for some weeks and truly is a joy and sense of accomplishment.

Farmers are looking for a good harvest also. God has answered our prayers by showing us that with His blessing, we can truly trust Him to do all that we have entrusted to His bountiful keeping. Not always does God answer our prayers as we would want. However, St. Paul writes at God's command: "All things work together for good to them that love God." (Romans 8:28).

It is no different in life for all of us. Sometimes we get more from life than we put into it, but, most frequently, it is what we put into life that we receive in return as a blessing from God. The gardener can receive much from his or her efforts, or, if nothing is done to care for the garden, they receive weeds. The farmer can prepare the soil and plant the seed and care for the crop and, with the blessing of God, receive a rich harvest.

So it is in life. When we give life our best effort using the talents God has given us, we receive a rich reward in the form of some material or spiritual blessing. We sometimes receive pain along with the good however. At times we may think God is wrong, but it is not God who is wrong, only our understanding of what we perceive. My friends, trust the Lord in all things and when you have traveled along life's path and reached either a turning point or its end, you can look back and say all things did work together for good "to them that love God." In the meantime, let us trust God and put our best into life. Accept the responsibility for it and live in peace with yourself, your family, your neighbors, and all else.

God is indeed good and loving and caring. Trust God in all things and you will receive the bounty of a loving God, perhaps not as you would wish, but it will be there. Remember Ecclesiastes chapter three: "God has made everything beautiful in its time...."

Fog

This past spring and summer we have had at times a great deal of fog, sometimes locally and other times generally, affecting all of us in one way or another. It makes driving difficult and we can't do much else outdoors either. Dispositions are affected and some experience a great deal of depression and confusion. Fog brings little excitement to our daily lives.

As with fog, so do issues in life. People don't always speak clearly and we can't know what they mean leaving us feel very confused. As with speech, so does the behavior of people. Thus, comes the expression, "I feel left out in the fog."

For your peace of mind and happiness, this need not be. There is one Who never left anyone in the fog with His Words and with His actions and that someone is Jesus. Friend, if you have a difficult situation in your life that makes you feel like you are living in the fog, then it is time to turn all of your life over to Jesus. He has said very clearly: "I am the Way, the Truth, and the Life." (John 14:6a). If you are having great difficulty in your life with family or friends or work, He has the way for you to seek out and follow; if you are having difficulty in your marriage, He has the way and the truth to resolve that conflict; if you are having difficulty at work, the Lord Jesus has the solution that will make it much more simple and peaceful for you to get through the day.

Many are the times, as the old commercial says."but ____, I'd rather do it myself," meaning we don't want help and would rather do it our own way. We can see more clearly to resolve our problems when the "Son" of God shines in our lives with His love and guidance. You can live life without Him and continue walking in the "fog," or you can turn the matter over to Him and live with far more peace and clarity. Ecclesiastes three says, "God has made everything beautiful in its time." Let's not blame God for the problems we have in our lives, but turn to Him to find the answers that bring true and lasting happiness which will see us through. There are no short cuts.

Up or Down!?

In our daily lives there are continuous up" and "downs" which are the concern for all involved. What happens around us and what people do to us or around us in our community always affects us positively or negatively.

To be sure, in the course of normal living, we will always have those "up" and downs," but those inflicted through carelessness or thoughtlessness by those around us are especially painful. There is always an effect from everything that is done whether good or bad. Sometimes we can do something about it. Other times we can only let others help us by doing it for us.

Let's look at community pride for example. One needs only to look around to see pride in many quarters. The appearance of the yards of our neighborhood, the neatness of the city streets, the attitudes of those living in the community all reflect the "up" and "downs" of the community. Look at self-respect for example. If one is unkempt, if one has a tendency to put one's self down, if one is determined to do what they want come "'hell' or high water" not considering what it does to others, this too, reflects upon the "up" and "downs" of life with devastating effect.

Our Lord said that we are to "love our neighbor as yourself." Do you think He has something to say to us today? How we treat others and how they treat us is reflective of a healthy life, a healthy community, or a sick life and a sick community. I ask all in one's community to do some soul searching. Let petty grievances be set aside for the good of all. Sometimes being right can have the effect of being wrong. Let all respect each other and work for the good of all. This comes out of self-sacrificing love. Christ set the example for us, and more, He paid the price so that we all can live in peace and love. If the Lord could forgive us, is it not time for all to forgive one another? Whoever you are, let changes begin today or we will be absorbed in self-destruction. The Bible says "A house divided against itself will fall." When there are "ups" and downs" in life, we begin to see them as the norm and not the abnormal. To paraphrase a line from a song: "Let there be love on earth and let it begin with me!"

Children

Children, to most people, are a precious gift from God, or, rather, should we say parents are a gift to children. Proverbs 17:6 says: "Children's children are a crown to the aged, and parents are the pride of their children." Many of us have good and precious memories of our childhood because we were loved. Some children have no happy memories from their childhood or home, and that is the saddest of tragedies.

In some cultures children have little meaning to their biological parents other than a possession and in those cultures children are sold for whatever reason. In some cultures homeless children are murdered by police "death squads" because they "threaten" those around them because of their rags and illnesses. Today, some children are murdered outright by means of abortion because they happened out of selfish and sinful abuse of sex and they became a burden to the selfish lives of those who conceived them.

Jesus had a very high regard for children. In fact, children were used by Jesus to teach adults how they should act in life and toward God. Adults are very difficult learners. When children are in school parents place an awesome responsibility upon the teacher to whom authority has thereby been given to aid in the raising of the their child. We take our hats off to those parents who work closely with the teachers of our school children. Let parents take time to work with their children and get to know their child as their own unique identity. Never should one be set at odds with the other. Only the child suffers.

Would that all parents could willingly and lovingly see how beautiful their children are. Perhaps then we would not have the problems today we are experiencing in our society. As Jesus loved children, so let us all love our children as a precious trust from God, and let us accept the responsibility of helping the child to grow to adult life and then accepting the responsibility of life and their place in society. Our Lord Jesus Christ has shown us the way. Let us follow His example. God says in the Holy Scriptures, "And you, fathers, provoke not your children to wrath, but bring them up in the nurture and admonition of the Lord." (Ephesians 6:4)

Giving Up

We get so tired in life that often we are tempted to simply "give up" and let whatever happen just happen. Children try so hard to please their peers, parents, and teachers, and never can, so they finally give up. Young adults give up when it seems that all the doors to advancement and success appear to be closed after they have given their best. Parents find it so difficult that some give up and let their youth do their "own thing," whatever that might be. When healthy people are ill over a long period of time, they give up when there seems to be no recovery taking place in their lives. The elderly often give up when it appears all others have no time for them. This list could be much longer, but we get the picture, don't we?

There is an answer to all of the above and more. St. Paul said it best when he said, "I can do all things through Christ Who strengthens me." The Gospel writer said it well when he wrote these words, "The gates of hell shall not prevail against you." Personally, Hebrews means so much that nothing else seems important. The writer said, "We have One Who was tempted (tested) in all ways as we, yet without sin." Nothing in our lives can be so great and impossible when we put it in the hands of the man Who can still even the waters, Jesus Christ Himself.

This calls for a great deal of trust and faith in One we cannot see, but, who nevertheless is with us always. We can always turn to Him and He will see us through.

Lay whatever is causing you grief in His arms and let Him carry the burden for you, guide you to the decision you need, and free you from grief that seems unbearable. The Lord loves you with a sacrificial love which will always see you through and give you the blessing of your heavenly Father. He will see you through even the darkest of days. This means you must walk by faith and trust in Him Who loves you so dearly that He gave you His best, Himself. Friend, don't give up, only live on with Him who is at your side and who will see you through. Remember the verse mentioned before: "I can do all things through Christ Who strengthens me," so that you do not have to give up.

Life

Life is one of the most precious gifts God has given all of His creation. Every plant, every insect, every animal, and all people, young and old, diligently hold on to life. When any part of a living thing or person is injured, built-in mechanisms immediately begin to promote healing and survival. Frequently we forget this truth and disregard the value of life with our actions.

We cut down old trees which are still healthy simply because they get in the way, forgetting the history and the contribution to our happiness that the tree has provided over the years. Trees are "bull-dozed" down and burned at random to make more land available for producing more of whatever we plant, or to make room for whatever we want to build. The same would hold true similarly of all things (and sometimes people) in our lives.

More and more, we are seeing utter disregard for human life in the movies we watch, and in the lives we live among others around us because we fight for our "rights." Life is not ours to do with as we feel. There are some guidelines for life and living, namely, respect, honor, and responsibility for all life. Life is God's precious gift to you and me. He makes each day more pleasant for those entrusted to us with the treasures He presents to us.

What would make for a happier life is a little slower pace of living that we might "take time to smell the roses." Why not enjoy the "simplest" of blessings that God has bestowed upon us? When we serve as we would be served, life takes on purpose and meaning and a sense of fulfillment and direction. When we take time to see the smallest of God's gifts to us, such as a little flower almost hidden in the grass or among the shrubs, we see the touch of the hand of God in a way that would help us re-evaluate our lives. Perhaps if more people took the time to see life as God created, there wouldn't be time for war, and murder, and all the other sordid things people do to each other. Enjoy life at all levels within the perimeters God created, and you will be surprised at the quality of your life.

It's Here

That little phrase can mean so much to so many people. We say it when we find something that has been lost. We use it when we have been driving and finally arrive at what we had thought was our destination and now find out is true existence. So many other times we find use for these two simple words it in our daily life; "it's here."

There are those who are searching for something in their lives and never seem to find it, always hoping to be able to say, "It's here," but never do. However, there are some who do find what they are looking for and are happy when "it" is found.

That little phrase is so non-descript, so seemingly unimportant, and yet, it is at the heart of all we do. Take, for example, our jobs. We keep striving for something better in the line of a raise, a promotion, a better location to work, better benefits, and much more. Or, Look at our schooling: we keep working for goals, and we achieve those goals by the best of grades possible. In our relationship with God some people find it almost immediately due to the influence of another person in their lives. Others seem to look for or wait for or put off indefinitely plans to live, and one wonders if they will ever find the "it" they are looking for with regard to God.

Well, if you are looking for the "it" of life, you will find "it" only with one person and that person is Jesus Christ, our Lord and Savior as revealed in the Scriptures and the path He would have us travel. He said he was "the Way, the Truth, and the Life" and for me that is "it." We can say to all people that life in its fullest sense is found here with the Lord Jesus Christ Himself. Here, with Him, there is meaning, there is purpose, there is fulfillment. If you are looking for "it," we can truthfully say to you, "It's Here" with Jesus. Trust Him, you won't find "it" in whatever you are looking for anywhere else. Begin your finding by reading the Gospel of St. John. There remains a great gift waiting for you in His Word at Jesus' feet.

Holy Week

The Gamut

This week throughout Christendom the whole gamut of Christ's purpose here on earth is remembered as being fulfilled from birth to death to the resurrection. Almost like a roller coaster, we see the life of Christ unfold before our very eyes. Holy Week, for this writer, is a time of personal introspection. Join with me as we look at the life, work and purpose of this one called Jesus of Nazareth.

Three and one half months ago we celebrated the birth of the Son of God, born of Mary, in a stable in Bethlehem. Eight days later He is presented in the temple where we hear aged Simeon and likewise aged Anna speaking words that foretell the life of this child called Jesus. It is sometime within the first two years of His life that His parents have to flee with Him to Egypt to save Him from King Herod and his murdering of the innocents (all male children two years of age and younger). At the age of twelve He appears in the temple speaking with the learned doctors of theology words portraying wisdom beyond a boy of His age. And, then, at about the age of thirty He is pointed out by John the Baptist to be the Lamb of God Who will take away the sins of the world. At the approximate age of 33, He is crucified simply because He loved so much.

During this Holy Week we recall the price Jesus paid for the sins of the whole world, the world of all ages, the world of all people from the East, from the West, from the North, and from the South. All because God loved and still loves you and me with an undaunted love, a love that is immeasurable by human standards. We hear Him cry out after having been crucified, "Father, forgive them for they know not what they do." Words that penetrate to this day the souls of the penitent. Words that comfort those carrying a heavy burden. Then, among others, He cries out, "It is finished." All that needed to be done to save you and me was now completed, it was done, it was finished. But, it still wasn't over. On the third day when the women went to the tomb, He was not there; and the angel explained it in this way: He, for Whom you look, is not here; He has risen as He said. Go tell the others."

The third day after the crucifixion we celebrate not a God Who is dead, not a Savior Whose body still lies in the grave as all religions of the world say of their god and savior, but a God and Savior Who lives as even the ancient archives of Rome have recorded in addition to what is recorded in Scripture. A Savior Who has conquered sin, death, and the devil. A Savior Who has met all that the only God of heaven and earth required of fallen man that he might live. Let all who hear this believe with all their heart as God invites you in Jesus today to do so. May all attend a house of worship of their choice where Jesus Christ is proclaimed in undaunted fervor and zeal: "Jesus Christ is risen, He is risen indeed!" Hallelujah! This is the gamut, from joy to the deepest depths of grief to ecstasy, the Christian passes through this week, with peace in and for his or her soul. Believe this, and you shall live.

Post Easter

Victory

Victory is desired by all ages in our encounters with life and in those matters that are important at the time. In school, victory is desired and worked hard for in sports, as we want to win the game and all work as a team to accomplish that goal. In such a sought after victory, all must do their part. Likewise one's goals in education are considered as worth of effort to accomplish and thus attain a kind of victory. When one is ill, the illness becomes that which we want to win over in our struggles to regain health.

There was another victory sought after and accomplished and won by Christ Jesus, the risen Lord and Savior. His enemies were and to this day are in our lives: sin, death, and the devil. Most Christians have just celebrated Easter. We attended worship services and met with family and friends and were renewed in our daily struggles to keep on striving for the victory, namely, to live in peace with man and God and to personally win the battle over sin, death and the devil in our own lives. All this by the message of the Word focused on Jesus Christ. This is the greatest victory of all for us to win. What would we do without Christ in our daily lives? Some appear to get by, but the time comes when the battle will not end and one ultimately comes to the realization that Christ is needed to have peace for daily living.

That is why Christ Jesus came. In our lives we can attain the final and ultimate victory through our Lord Jesus Christ by believing in Him. Here is the strength for daily living, for peace within and with one's self. Here is our hope for tomorrow. Here is our strength to carry our cross, whatever that may be either for now, or, perhaps yet to come. Here is our focus for life when all goes well and we always recognize and thank God from whom and from where it has come. The child of God can always say "Christ is risen indeed" and find its fulfillment in all of the blessings that come from the hand of a loving and caring God Who makes possible the way to and the receiving of the crown of victory itself in Christ Jesus our Lord.

Post Easter

Easter Over?

Or, is it? Some think that Easter is over: the stores have removed their candy and "stuff;" guests have gone home; diets are renewed; and the churches "special services" are over and we return to normal every week worship and the routine of everyday living. For these, Easter is over.

The disciples made an adjustment after Easter. The fact of seeing One who was dead but was now showing Himself alive to many different people changed their lives profoundly. They saw the wounds in His hands, feet and side; but His eating, resting and teaching, and doing many of those things which He had done before the awe-filled days of His crucifixion and then His resurrection were a little difficult for the followers of Jesus to handle. First, they didn't know why He had come because they, like the rest, looked for an earthly ruler. Second, they didn't understand their place in His plans for them in His kingdom.

Much hasn't changed for today. Many living among us do not see their Savior in Christ, but rather just a "good guy," a great teacher, another one who has not done much for them, at least in their terms, and is still in the grave. Christ Jesus is the only Savior Who has risen from the dead and is not in the grave as are all other "leaders" man has invented and concocted. Christ Jesus is no stone statue, no dead leader, but the living and only true God. For others, this day is seen as a time of rejoicing because, by faith in Christ Jesus as their personal Savior, they can overcome all that would hurt them in some way. They know that the "grave" is not the end, but only the beginning. Some see Christ Jesus with great joy, as the One who is with them as He promised and does give them strength to overcome all that attacks them daily. Others see Christ Jesus as the One who walks with them through the valley of the shadow of death. All find peace in the finished act of God to make full payment for their sins to set them free to live for Him in freedom and peace and joy and love and understanding with a future that is forever bright.

Easter isn't over! It has only just begun. We now live in the afterglow of the warmth of God's love and peace and acceptance into His Family once again through Christ Jesus. Friend, rejoice, God is not dead, but lives for you! In return, live for Him! If you haven't given your life to Him, do so today and join the millions who follow a Savior that loves them and will love them until they stand before Him in Heaven. Christ is risen, Alleluia! And He lives for you!

Hosanna - Palm Sunday

Hosanna

"Hosanna" is what was shouted and sung in praise almost 2000 years ago when Jesus entered Jerusalem. Children and adults lined the streets to welcome the One, who, at least in their eyes, could feed the hungry, heal the sick, raise the dead, and do all kinds of miracles which made peoples' lives a little easier under the Roman occupation. People saw what they wanted to see.

Is it any different today? People see what they want to see as long as it directly or indirectly serves their own end in life regardless of the cost to whomever. In this holy season of Lent as it nears its close with the coming of Holy Week and its culmination in the festival of the Resurrection, we are called to reflect upon ourselves in every way possible. When, as in many churches, the children confess their faith and are confirming the same on Palm Sunday, let us all search our own hearts for that which the Lord would have us find there. Do we find faith, a saving faith in Jesus Christ as our personal Savior, a living and active faith, a faith that daily puts into practice what we so easily can say with our mouths. Let us make in this time of Holy Week a commitment anew of self, body and soul, to our Lord Jesus Christ.

Let us sing our "Hosannas" to our Lord and King, Jesus Christ, who came that God's law might be fulfilled in our stead. In the words of Jesus, "I have come so that you might have life and have it to the fullest." Jesus also said, "I am the Way, the Truth, and the Life. No man comes unto the Father but by Me." We do have good cause to sing and shout our "Hosannas" to the only living Lord and

God of heaven and earth, the only One that can fulfill our lives in its riches sense, the only true sense.

As we celebrate Palm Sunday, Holy Week, and Easter, let us celebrate with a sense of humility and awe and sincere faith through deep commitment to the one and only God of heaven and earth, Jesus Christ. Let us in sincere faith sing our hosannas to the Song of God, the only One Who alone can give meaning and purpose to our everyday lives.

Fall
Fallen Leaves

Fall is an interesting time of the year. We see so many changes around us with one season giving way for another. So much life is seen illustrated for us by God's creation. We remember the words of Scripture, which say that there will always be seasons. (Ecclesiastes 3:1). From this, we can learn a simple lesson. Everything has its place and everything has its purpose.

Life is like this. We are born, and this is spring. We begin our lives not knowing what they will develop into because of all the variables that surround us. And as a paraphrase of the Scriptures says, "As the twig is bent, so grows the tree." We see young lives grow and develop for the Summer of life. These are the productive years. Our lives again are predictive of the end product. Our Lord said, "By their fruits you shall know them." Summer gives way to Fall, the harvest. At this time in life we see the results of many years of hard labor, and we can "enjoy the fruits of our labors." Then comes winter, the time of rest and restoration. Some see this as a dreaded time, but with God this is a beautiful time, a time when all that are His in Christ Jesus rest with Him. These all are beautiful times in the lives of all, or at least should be.

This puts the responsibility of living upon each of our shoulders. We cannot give that away to anyone else nor entrust that to anyone else.

Let us all take time to take in God's beauty in the midst of these troubled times. God has only His best in store for you; and when that time comes, we shall be blest with the richest of His blessings. Let us live with faith in Christ and perseverance and trust in His love and presence, and His gift of the real life will be ours forever.

Winter
Let It Snow

The forecast often this winter is SNOW, but, then, this is winter, right? What else can we expect in winter? Snow in its time and place is beautiful. Snow covers the dirt and fallen leaves and whatever else we have thrown on the ground. Snow makes all beautiful because we can't see the drab or whatever we wish to call that which produces depression, anxiety, "down in the mouth" feelings. When this season sets in, psychiatrists report more patients, as is also the case of spring. Change is very difficult for some people.

Change, for us, is difficult at any time, isn't it? We must get used to something different from what has provided security in our lives and the lives of those close to us. What makes change resented most of all is when someone attempts to give us a "snow job," that is, when someone says one thing and means another, acting as if we are too dumb to know better. When this is done to us, that kind of "snow" is not beautiful even though it covers something up and appears to give the appearance of something more palatable to our lives.

What we need today are fewer "snow jobs" and more honesty and truth in our lives, not only from those around us, but also from ourselves. Children need the simple truth from their parents, teachers and community. Individuals need the outright truth to build secure lives for themselves and those around them. We need to be treated with respect and honor. How lives would change if more people were given fewer "snow jobs" and more truth.

For this to happen, "let it begin with me." The Lord tells us that the simple "truth" is the foundation of life. Jesus said, "I am the Way, the Truth, and the Life." May our lives find their fulfillment in every way with Jesus, who is the Truth. When this happens, there will be no "snow jobs" and our lives will be much more acceptable and less anxious about any change whatever it may involve. Let us all enjoy our lives with Christ as the center of life, for His love covers all things. Let snow (the white stuff) always be a reminder of the beauty of life with Christ whose blood makes us as clean as snow in forgiveness and sincerity out of a heart that sincerely loves us, no matter what we may have done.

Cold

Winter is the time for cold weather. We dress ourselves warmer adapting ourselves to the temperature, and we make the best of it. We talk about it and sometimes we complain about it and others still talk about it with satisfaction because they are involved in the winter activities. Whatever we do, it is our perspective that shapes our response.

Sad, yes, tragic, is the "cold" people experience in their lives because of the attitudes and perception of others. No one wants to be left out in the "cold," that is, separated from others in the community. No one wants to be treated "coldly," by friends and neighbors. We all need one another whether all are ready to admit it or not. There should be no place in our lives to treat anyone with a "cold" attitude for whatever we perceive as the reason.

In God's family there is an acceptance of all in Christ Jesus the Lord. No greater Friend could one wish or desire than Jesus Christ. Jesus never treated any man, woman or child in need of love "coldly." He healed the sick, raised the dead, forgave sinners and spent time with the lonely. Instead of "cold," there was sincere "warmth" and acceptance. That's what we all need. That's what we all have in Him. We sing "What a Friend we have in Jesus, All our sins and griefs to bear, What a privilege to carry Everything to God in Prayer. Oh, what peace we often forfeit, Oh, what needless pain we bear, All because we do not carry Everything to God in prayer." Let us turn to Him now and find acceptance and warmth from the "cold" for all eternity through Him in our heavenly Father's family.

Let us be more "warm" to all those around us then and not "cold." This is the beginning of peace, of fulfillment, and of a life of completeness. Lord, let it begin with me.

Christmas

Each of us holds something sacred in our hearts, something that warms our innermost being when we think of Christmas under any circumstance. For me Christmas holds such a place dear in my heart. Christmases past recall for me memories as a child, a teenager, a student in college and the seminary, a young adult, a newly married, a young parent, a parent of a teenager, a parent of newly married children, a grandparent, and now a great grandparent. What is sacred has remained with me throughout the years, and it will always be kept in my heart for my enrichment as you would and do keep yours. This is what traditions are made of. Thank God for the good things that build our lives so richly to give them meaning.

Indeed, thank God. Thank God for the gift of His Son, Jesus Christ. God loves us so much that He could not stop short of this His most precious gift. He counted the cost and still He gave freely to us. What is sad is that so many don't acknowledge this precious gift as personal in their own hearts and lives and lock Him out. We won't spend time on all that seems to be going wrong, for that would be pointless. Let us gather around as family and celebrate this warmth of Christ's love glowing in our hearts, a love that is not self-centered but out going, a love that truly has its roots in the Lord Jesus Christ.

God did that on that first Christmas when His Son was born of the Virgin Mary in Bethlehem. From then on, there was a cord between Himself and all men, women, and children, that we could see and listen to and follow and commit to. This is where the real Christmas was established and is for all eternity. It is from here the message was renewed and fulfilled of peace possible on earth as announced again by the angels. It was at this time that man was again told not to be afraid.

It is my prayer that all would come to know Christ the Lord as Savior and Friend. That all would build their Christmases around Him for that which lasts and adds beauty and meaning to our very existence. Let me share these word from a most beloved hymn about this real meaning of Christmas:

Joy to the world, the Lord has comes,
Let earth receive her king;
Let every heart prepare Him room,
And heaven and nature sing, And heaven and nature sing,
And heaven, and heaven and nature sing.

Have a Christmas blest by God in His Son, Jesus Christ and may your future find eternal meaning in your relationship with Him.

Christmas
Miracle

Do you believe in miracles? I do! Miracles happen every day around us and to us. The gift of family for those who have a family and that includes just about every one of us. If Christ lives with the single person who has no family here on earth, that is family and the gift is even greater. The gift of health we have even though it may be limited allows us still to enjoy what we do have left in this life with Christ beside us. The list goes on. The greatest gift of all is God giving us His only Son, Jesus Christ, on that first Christmas almost 2,000 years ago. This enabled St. Paul later to say with conviction, "I can do all things through Christ Who strengthens me," and also these words of Paul, "neither death, nor life, nor principalities, nor powers, nor things to come, nor height, nor depth, nor any other creature shall be able to separate us from the love of God which is in Christ Jesus, our Lord." Now that is a miracle among miracles.

When we celebrate Christmas think for one minute what Christmas truly means. It means that God worked the greatest miracle of all, namely, the birth of His Son. Jesus was conceived by a miracle of the Holy Spirit with the Virgin Mary. He was born as you and I were born. Jesus grew up in the home of His parents Mary and Joseph and learned to love, respect, obey and honor them. He studied the Word of His heavenly Father to the degree that He could sit and discuss Bible teaching with the doctors of theology in the temple at the age of 12. He became involved in the lives of people about the age of 30 at the wedding in Cana and throughout the next three years. He was tempted in every way that we are, yet, He did not commit one solitary sin. His only love was that we would live with Him in Heaven for all eternity and for this He willingly died on the cross in our place. Christmas is from conception to the resurrection and beyond "that we might have life and have it abundantly." My friend, believe this with all your heart and you shall live. Celebrate this Christmas with Christ as your guest and you shall never be the same again.

You are invited to worship Him every weekend in the Christian Church near you to celebrate this great miracle. Come, for you are welcome in the Family of God. Now, all this is a true miracle especially for you.

Christmas

Inquisitiveness

It seems that this time of the year always arouses the inquisitive minds of everyone. Children become more aware of the actions of their parents as they watch for some sign of the Christmas gifts they will receive. They look for hiding places for their gifts they have for those they love and the hiding place for the gift which was lovingly purchased for them. As adults, we wonder if we will get a pay raise, if we will have a good winter for the Christmas festivities, if we will have a good Christmas celebration. We wonder if next year will be a better year than this year. And so the list goes on and on.

There is nothing wrong with an inquisitive mind. The old adage of "curiosity killed the cat" doesn't "hold water" in our lives. Curiosity always leads to the expanding of the mind and heart, for only in this way do we grow in our knowledge, in our family, in our community, and in our own individual lives.

The inquisitive shepherds went to Bethlehem to see that which the angels had talked about. The wise men from the East journeyed to Bethlehem in search of what they knew to have happened according to the sacred scriptures. And Mary "kept all these things" (that which the angel had told her) and "wondered about them in heart." Herod too was inquisitive but for another reason for all this he saw a threat to his throne.

We need to be inquisitive at all times. Otherwise, we will be covered with mold from a form of death worse than death itself.

Self satisfaction is the death of all that is good. Let us hold to the curiosity, the inquisitiveness of a child, this Christmas and always our lives will be filled with challenge, satisfaction, and fulfillment.

Christ is what Christmas is all about. Other that this, you will have just another "hum-drum" holiday with the usual holiday hang-overs. Let inquisitiveness lead you to the manger to worship the King, Jesus Christ, that you may know Jesus Christ as "the Way, the Truth, and the Life" for this life and for that life which is yet to come. Happy inquisitiveness!

Christmas

Home

"Home is where the heart is," or, at least this is what they say. As we come close to the holiday season we hear of more and more efforts being made to provide meals for the homeless, to gather toys for the homeless or poor children and much more, some of which does not honor Christ. One entertainer wanted to change a traditional holiday song "I'll be home for Christmas" to "I'll be home for Christmas (over) the cries of the homeless." It is not for me to judge the reason behind all these efforts, but it does remind me of the great treasure the Lord has provided for me and my family. We have a home to always come home to.

One person who changed the course of history never had a home. The verse in Scripture that included the phrase "He had no where to lay His head" takes on greater significance for me as we celebrate Christmas when one considers the depth of God's love for "the world." Each Christmas and the weeks before and after, all revolve around this gift of God which provides for you and me the gift of a "home."

Let us not take this home for granted. The phrase earlier referred to namely, "Home is where the heart is" has more truth in it than at first consideration. My home is where the Lord brings together first Himself and us; and second, where all gather together where we live; and third, where Christians gather for worship. That is a very well-rounded concept of home.

As the special observance of Christ's birthday comes upon us; and as we prepare for the second coming of Christ again at that day when He shall gather together all those who are His, we rejoice in our opportunities to give gifts to the homeless, to our friends, and to those near and dear to us, our family. Let us take the time to enrich someone's life with a measure of our love following the example of God Almighty in the gift of His Son that all could be home for Christmas. Let us all build warm and secure homes with Christ Jesus at the heart of all that we do this day and always.

Christmas
Destinations

Our lives are filled with destinations. We all are headed somewhere at sometime in our lives. We have certain places we want to be in our lives by certain times. It matters little with the age of the individual. Let's take a look at one person whose life was filled with destinations - The Son of God, Jesus Christ.

His destinations originate with the love of God. (John 3:16) His first destination was a stable to be born of the Virgin Mary. (Read the accounts of Jesus' birth in Matthew and Luke). This destination was reached in its final stage in the stable of Bethlehem, all according to prophecy as spoken by the prophet Micah. His next destination was Egypt (according to prophecy) to escape the hate of Herod and the "murder of the innocents." His next destination was Cana of Galilee where He intervened on behalf of the master of a great wedding feast and performed His first miracle. His many destinations following were in the lives of people who needed to know God's love in their Friend and Savior, Jesus Christ, Who forgave their sins, healed their sick, and did other great miracles to show that God cared for each and every one of His people no matter what their station in life. Other destinations of His were the cross, the grave, and the many appearances to so many different people after His resurrection. He then ascended into Heaven where He rules at the right hand of the heavenly Father until His final coming.

What does this all have to do with Christmas? It is the reason for Christmas. IT IS CHRISTMAS! Anything else falls short of a real Christmas.

Joy to the world, the Lord has come,
Let earth receive its King,
Let every heart, prepare Him room,
And heaven and nature sing,
And heaven and nature sing.
And heaven, and heaven and nature sing.

His one destination He desires most of all is your heart.

Resting

Resting is an experience which all need. This is the way we are made, that is, for a time of rest for body and mind. We need to be refreshed and strengthened from the past and for the future. That leaves us to make the most of this moment in which we live today.

All of creation is made this way. It was no different with God in the beginning of the creation. For six days God created the heavens and the earth and all that is in them, and then the Bible says He rested on the seventh. Perhaps today if we would all use this time to rest instead of whatever it is that we do which prevents us from resting we, would be a happier people.

Parents could spend so much more time with their children and the children with their parents is they would rest with each other. Now resting does not mean staying in bed. Resting means a diversion from what we do regularly, a change of pace, a different tempo. How beautiful it would be if families would rest by worshiping together in God's House weekly to begin the calendar week we call Sunday. How much more precious would our family time be if we spent some of it with each other in the Word and in prayer for one another and singing praises to Almighty God. Perhaps we would have more peace in the community and in the world if during this rest period, we would rest with each other in the quiet of each other's love and presence.

Jesus spent time resting on the mountainside, in the temple, on the lake, with His friends, and just walking with His disciples helping one another to face the future. Let us, during this time before

Christmas, take some time to rest and enter into the Christmas holy day with a calm and refreshed spirit in the Lord. R.I.P.

Help

It is safe to say that there is no one that can live without help at some point of time in the lives. Children need help from all those around them, even though our communities do all they can to provide that help for them. Teenagers need help even though they are expressing more and more independence they still need the help of those to whom their lives have been entrusted. Young adults, out on their own, find the need for help more quickly than they expected. Adults remember the past years of advice and counsel and, unknown to those who gave it, use that help everyday of their lives. (It's called applied knowledge). Middle-aged people begin to realize the need for help of a new kind as they approach retirement. And the golden agers are in the need of help and understanding from all those whom they have helped over the years.

Another kind of help is something other than physical. It's called spiritual. Spiritual help is our need for help from outside ourselves. We wish to identify the only one who can give this help and His name is Jesus. He came that "we might have life and have it more abundantly." (John 10:10) We all need to have a path to follow; and again Jesus provides that path to follow as He said, "I am the Way, the Truth, and the Life." (John 14:6). The Psalmist said "Your Word is a lamp unto my feet and a light unto my path." (Psalm 119:105). Over and over again, our loving and caring God has invited us to come to Him for Help.

During these weeks of preparation for the celebration of the birthday of Christ the King, let us help one another in every way possible that we all can enjoy a happy holiday every day of our lives.

Someone has said that the joy of Christmas is the giving, not the receiving. Let us all give of our hearts to everyone around us for we are all family in Christ. If you are in need of help, feel free to call a Christian church in your community. In these troubled times, we all need the help that only Jesus Christ can give us. The Lord said, "Call upon Me in the day of trouble and I will deliver you." This month, this Christmas, yes, for the rest of your life, call upon Jesus. As St. Paul said, "I can do all things through Christ Who strengthens me.

Is It Over or Just Beginning?

We've reached that point in time when we are in between the passing and the coming of time as told by calendar. This leaves many people with mixed feelings and emotions. Saddened by what was lost or changed, never to be again and gladdened by what is unknown but anticipated.

No one likes to be unsure of their place or situation in life. Our Lord has some wise words for all to consider. He said, "TRUST IN THE LORD WITH ALL YOUR HEART AND DO NOT DEPEND ON YOUR OWN UNDERSTANDING." (Proverbs 3:5) No wiser counsel could be given to us than this, whether we are anxious or content. Jesus also told His disciples to become as little children, that is, having the trust of a child. In these uncertain times may it be exactly that, trusting in the Lord for all that is before and around us for everyday living.

A little child, who had just entered the house with its father from a terrible storm outside, was asked, "Weren't you afraid?" To which the child replied immediately with a smile, "No, my daddy was holding me." Our Heavenly Father is holding and carrying us too, in this life of ours with all its uncertainties and unknowns. This, my friend, is in the hands of the Heavenly Father. Know this, that He loves us so much it cost Him His Son Jesus. Therefore, let us trust Him between the past and the future because, now, in the present, we are in His care. He shall give us the strength and the guidance and the peace needed from day to day even though we don't know what the day hold for us. All of the past, present and future is in His hands.

Have a New Year blest by God and a worry free passing from the old. You can't go wrong!

Wishes

This is the season for many, many wishes. If you don't believe me, just listen to the children, or listen to someone facing a decision or conflict or some such issue of every day life and you will hear any and all say, "I wish. . . ." We've spoken of the wish book before, but, now also, I say that this wish book is something all of us have for just getting through the day. We wish for less pain, less hurt, more friends, more happiness, more peace.

If such is your thinking there is good news for you. Many years ago angels came down from heaven and spoke to the shepherds who were watching their flocks by night and said, "Peace on earth and good will among men." God knew what was in the hearts of all people everywhere of all time. He knew of the desire for peace, for less hurting. That is why He gave us His Son to be born of a virgin that He might take our place and suffer the pain and take the hurt and forgive the sin of all.

Friend, this is not just a wish. This is an accomplished fact for you and for me. Nowhere will anyone find anything or anyone other than Jesus Christ, God's Son, that can bring so much peace of mind and heart. God knew exactly what He was doing when He sent His Son to be born of a Virgin in a lowly stable for you and me. No pretense here, just the sincere desire, the deepest love, to lift us up from the mess of living we so often find ourselves in whether by our own design or someone else's.

In this holy season AND AFTER, go to where the Savior can be found. Find a Christian Church in your community that shares this

Christ and with them find continuously that peace which will never again give you time to wish. You will have in Christ, the Lord of life, peace and love and hope and joy which cannot be found anywhere else. God's best to you, my friend.

Christmas

Anticipation

This is the season of anticipation for all ages. For some, it is waiting for relatives to come home, relatives they haven't seen for a long time, sons and daughters coming home for the holidays. Children are looking with innocent anticipation to the gifts they dream of receiving. Others look forward to the services in their church with the singing of carols and hymns giving praise to the King of Kings. Some, sadly so, look ahead and see only loneliness because they have no one to come for a visit, or no place to go and nothing, at least materially speaking, to give or expectantly to receive.

To all of every station in life, let me say this, "You have a friend, a companion, a Savior, Christ the Lord, the Gift which God Himself has given to you." He came because we were in need and He knew that the only way to make all things right for us was for Him to come and be as one of us, real flesh and blood, with all the human feelings, needs, and emotions which we experience regularly. He is the perfect gift of a Friend, and Companion, a Comforter, the Giver of Peace.

Let not this coming Christmas be emphasized by the number of gifts or friends you have or do not have, but with the joyous celebration of the birthday of Christ the King, your Savior and Friend. If you are all alone, we invite you to find a Christian Church near you which knows the Savior and celebrate with them the joyous giving by God of the greatest gift ever given to and for you and all people, namely, His Son, Jesus Christ. This Christmas celebrate in joyful remembrance of this great act of God's love, the giving of the Christ and His coming again to receive all who believe in Him as their personal Savior and Friend. Let this coming Christmas be the greatest of all.

To God belongs the glory. Anticipation: let it be that of joy and peace and hope in Christ for such times as these. God bless you and make your observance of Christmas one of thanksgiving for such an act and gift of love in Jesus Christ, His Son, Who came that you may have life and have it abundantly.

Graduation
Do We Ever Graduate?

Since the children have gone back to school, it brought to mind the title of this column for this week. People often live as if they have graduated from ever again taking the time to sit down and try to learn something new. This is called living in the past. Now, to be sure, there is nothing wrong with having good memories, but, this is different from living in the past. The person guilty of living in the past hardly ever wants to change anything no matter how much more blest their life could be if they would take the time to learn something new.

We can never stop learning. If we tried, we would fall short of the Lord's words which invite us to invest our talents in the matter of life. That's why we have them. How dull life would be if we stopped short of this with anything less than our best with which we have been gifted by God. Life challenges us today with the needs of people which seem to become ever greater as the days progress. That's why we never graduate from learning.

We can always learn to apply knowledge. "Wisdom" is the application of knowledge. Wisdom comes only from experience. The Bible says "the fear of the Lord is the beginning of wisdom." When we look around us, we can see that there is much to be learned and that this learning begins with the Lord and His way for our lives.

When Jesus said, "Follow Me," He meant in all that we say and do and think. When He is number one in our lives, then we will always be ready to learn from everyone around us and from everything around us and from all that happens in our lives. We will stop with nothing less than our best, and our best will be achieved only when we continue to learn, having committed our life to Christ.

With the Lord as the basis of life, then we truly will daily find peace and fulfillment and meaning for our lives. So the question, "Do We Ever Graduate?" No! As responsible people we never graduate, but continue to learn from mistakes as well as successes and thus come to enjoy real happiness! St. Paul said, "I can do all things through Christ who strengthens me."

Surprises

In all of our lives, there is the time when we experience "surprise" in one form or another. We are surprised when we enter a room and our family and friends are there waiting for us to enter that we might celebrate a birthday or some other special happening. We are surprised when we enter a room and someone is waiting there to scare us. We are surprised when we receive a gift that was waited for over such a long period of time that we were about to give up on that item. We are surprised when we wake up in the morning and look out the window and seen snow falling.

Surprise, by the unexpected, or by the long overdue expected, has always been a part of living. It's what we do with it which makes the difference between the positive and negative feelings and actions of our lives. We know of someone who reacts to surprise when we touch him in a physically dangerous way to our health. Children laugh with unabated expression when surprised. Some people even cry when they are surprised. We are always in touch with surprises.

Something that should never be a surprise for us is the love of the Lord Jesus Christ, especially when we "fall short of the mark." It is a gift from Him a treasure long awaited by some. Love is what He has for all if only we would receive it as He gives it. When you are at your darkest moment, He is there waiting for you with His love. We sing of this in the hymn: "What a Friend we have in Jesus, All our sins and griefs to bear, What a privilege to carry everything to him in prayer. Oh, what peace we often forfeit, Oh what needless pain we bear, All because we do not carry everything to

God in prayer." He is there waiting when we are experiencing a trial of a proportion that we feel we can no longer endure, for he says, "Call upon Me in the day of trouble and I will deliver you," and "Cast all your burdens upon Him for He cares for you." He will be there for us even when we leave this world, for He says by the psalmist, "Yea, though I walk through the valley of the shadow of death I will fear no evil, for Thou art with me." (Psalm 23:4). Also, "I go to prepare a place for you, and if I go and prepare a place for you I will come again and receive you unto myself, that where I am you will be also." (John 14:3). In this life, with God, there are no surprises! Trust Him and true life will be a satisfaction for you! Don't be surprised, God loves you!

Holy Week

Living

What does really living mean to you? A good house to live in? A comfortable bank account? A goodly number of friends? A place of honor in your community? When a survivor at a grave side saw the deceased being buried in a Cadillac, he was overheard to remark: "Now that's really living!" Somehow when we hear something like that, we get the feeling that some priorities are mixed up, to say the least.

It was no different in Jesus' time. People were looking for an earthly king and when Jesus came and was heard to say to the throngs of people that followed Him His purpose was not to be an earthly king, the people left Him by the same number so that on the night before His death He met only with His twelve disciples of whom even one of the betrayed Him.

Who or what is Jesus to you? He came that we might have life and have it abundantly. (John 10). He said that we were to take up our cross and follow Him. (Mark 8). His way was, as is ours, the way of denial of self (Matthew 16). In the eyes of the world and many around us, these statements are words of failure. According to them, one wouldn't say that you were really living.

WRONG! This Holy Week we once again focus very personally on the real "living" that is there for all. Christ is very personal, and Christ is very real. He wants all to know this. On Thursday evening many Christians will celebrate the Lord's Supper, commonly referred to as the "Last Supper" of Jesus. We have this New Covenant with God and from God, in which He renews His personal words of kinship and living with and for all. On Good Friday we gather together to we commemorate His death on the cross for all those things we fail in doing by thought, word, and deed. We enter into a time of reflection upon our "living" and bring it into compliance with that of the Lord Jesus Christ.

AND THEN ON EASTER MORNING WE CELEBRATE THE GREATEST VICTORY EVER IN THE HISTORY OF MAN! There are some who have great difficulty speaking of death, but what they fail to see is that beyond death (because of Christ's "living") is life for all who would have it for themselves. This life is in Christ Jesus the Lord and is yours simply by believing it! Humbly accept that truth in faith without any reservation or doubt. With Christ Jesus the Living Lord, you can really live. My friend, go to a truly Christian Church that knows Christ personally and celebrate what Jesus calls really "living." In Christ there is no loss, no defeat, no end, BUT ONLY LIVING. Take Time to worship with your spiritual brothers and sisters that One Who rules in life this day.

Index

Special Days

Memorial Day	Page 33
Do We Ever Graduate	Page 136

Holy Days: Christmas

Anticipation	Page 135
"Christmas"	Page 117
Destinations	Page 125
Home	Page 123
Inquisitiveness	Page 121
Miracle	Page 119

Holy Days: Lent

Afraid	Page 1
Crown of Thorns and Glory	Page 65
Good	Page 5
Hosanna	Page 109
Living I	Page 73
Living II	Page 141
The Gamut	Page 103

Holy Days: Easter

Easter Lives	Page 69
Easter Over?	Page 107
Victory	Page 105
Routine	Page 71
Spring/Life	Page 57

General

Anxious	Page 3
Caring	Page 9
Children	Page 95
Cold	Page 115
Company	Page 87
Deliverer	Page 11
Discouraged	Page 13
Dissatisfied	Page 15
Evening	Page 81
Fallen Leaves	Page 111
Fog	Page 91
Friendly	Page 37
Friends	Page 85
Forgiveness	Page 17
Fruits of Life	Page 89
Giving Up	Page 97
Guilty	Page 19
Help	Page 129
Hurt	Page 53
Integrity	Page 21
It's Here	Page 101
Is It All Over or Just Beginning	Page 131
Laugh	Page 31
Let It Snow	Page 113
Life	Page 99
Life With Meaning	Page 79
Play	Page 27
Quiet Time	Page 75
Rain	Page 49
Read	Page 29
Resting	Page 127
Relationships	Page 63
Responsibility	Page 67
Sunrise	Page 83
Surprises	Page 139
The Guide	Page 47

Think	Page 39
Time-Off	Page 35
The Lowly Sparrow	Page 61
Thoughtfulness	Page 55
Trim	Page 51
Trouble	Page 43
Trust	Page 77
Weather	Page 45
Wishes	Page 133
Work	Page 23
Worship	Page 41

www.ingramcontent.com/pod-product-compliance
Lightning Source LLC
Chambersburg PA
CBHW051102230426
43667CB00013B/2408